200

GETTIN

CW00434957

LAW

THIRD EDITION

991864804 X

Getting into Law, third edition

This third edition published in 1999
by Trotman and Company Ltd
2 The Green, Richmond, Surrey TW9 1PL

© Trotman and Company Limited 1999

British Library Cataloguing in Publication Data
A catalogue record for this book is available from the
British Library.

ISBN 0 85660 455 0

Printed and bound in Great Britain
by Creative Print & Design (Wales) Ltd

CONTENTS

PREFACE

Over the past few years the number of applicants to the legal profession has increased enormously.

In MPW's work of advising would-be students on their choice of university course, we have gathered together a huge amount of information on law courses and the legal profession. With the encouragement of Trotman & Company this information has been brought together in this guide.

I am very grateful to all the contributors and I hope that the guide will be of use wherever eager school and college pupils, as well as mature students and those considering changing their career, want to know more about getting into law.

Nigel Stout
MPW
June 1999

ACKNOWLEDGEMENTS

This third edition of *Getting into Law* has been extensively revised and updated by **Fiona Hindle**, an independent careers consultant. For many years she has worked at the University of London Careers Service, providing careers advice to students and graduates in the Faculty of Law at University College London. She specialises in providing full careers consultancy to individuals and employers in the legal profession.

This book was originally the work of a number of contributors without whose specialist knowledge it would not have been born. Thanks go to the following:

Dr James Holland, Associate Dean (Academic Studies) in the Faculty of Law at the University of the West of England in Bristol. He is also the co-author of *Learning Legal Rules* published by Blackstone Press.

Joanne Hubert works as a legal and financial information researcher.

Mike Semple Piggot was chief executive of the BPP Law School – one of the independent colleges that provide postgraduate legal education. He has set up an innovative virtual law school on the Internet which you can access on http://www.sppa.co.uk. **Frances Burton** has also provided some valuable comments.

Julian Webb, Director of Postgraduate Programmes in the Faculty of Law at the University of the West of England. He co-wrote *Learning Legal Rules* with Dr Holland.

Paul Whiteside studied History at both University College London and Queen Mary & Westfield College before completing a Diploma in Law at City University and attending the College of Law. For over ten years he has been teaching Law and social sciences at undergraduate and A-level.

INTRODUCTION

WHAT THIS BOOK IS ABOUT

Unless this book has just slipped off the shelf into your hands and fallen open at this very page, you're probably reading it hoping to pick up some pearls of wisdom on whether or not you should study law. Well, read on... This guide is intended to answer those questions you've always wanted to ask and possibly a few more that have never crossed your mind.

Broadly, there are three sections in this book:

1. First, there's a brief introduction to the legal profession, followed by a description of what solicitors and barristers actually do and how they fit into the scheme of the legal system.

2. There follows a selection of ways in which you can become a solicitor or a barrister, including how to get work experience, and some flow charts to summarise that information.

3. The remainder of the book is dedicated to guiding you through the vast range of law courses on offer.

Don't be fooled, however, into thinking that *Getting into Law* will do all the work for you so you can put your feet up and watch 'The Bill' on TV!

You will still have to...

■ Revise thoroughly and pass your exams. You can get on to a few university courses with fairly low grades, but those courses might not suit your needs. You'd be better off with higher grades and a wider choice of degree options available to you.

1

You should also…

- Do your own research. Talk to your teachers, friends, family, legal practitioners – anyone who might know something about the legal profession. Consider carefully what type of course is appropriate for you. Or, come to that, whether you should even think about studying law in the first place.

Chapter 1 AN INTRODUCTION TO THE LEGAL PROFESSION

Your first impression of the legal profession may be via film or television. Go on, admit it – how many of you would secretly like to be Kavanagh, Ally McBeal or one of the glamorous young lawyers living life in the fast lane in 'This Life'. You'll have seen barristers in court robed in wig and gown, confidently destroying a witness with one telling question. Equally, you will be familiar with the sight of the solicitor's office in the high street where wills are drafted or houses conveyed. But what are the differences between barristers and solicitors (other than the barristers' novel dress sense)? And where do lawyers and attorneys come into it?

Well, the legal profession in England and Wales is a split profession. Solicitors are like general practitioners in the medical profession. They have direct and continuing contact with their clients and deal with many different aspects of the law, not just those that end up in court.

Barristers are more like consultants or surgeons. Their main function is to wield the scalpel on behalf of clients referred to them by solicitors, and they may often only meet their clients on the day of trial.

So solicitors and barristers should be seen as operating within a loose team, performing different but interdependent roles. The term 'lawyer' is simply a collective term for barristers, solicitors, judges, some civil servants, academic lawyers and even law undergraduates; whereas the word 'attorney' refers to American lawyers and means nothing in English law. This book concentrates on the distinct types of work undertaken by barristers and solicitors.

It is also worth noting that the Scottish legal profession is distinct from that of England and Wales, although there is an equivalent division of the profession between solicitors and advocates (the term used for barristers in Scotland). Solicitors belong to the Law Society of Scotland; advocates are collectively referred to as 'The Bar' and belong to the Faculty of Advocates. Legal education, legal traditions, the courts and legal language in Scotland are quite different from those used in English law.

So, although there are many similarities between practising north or south of the border, the comments below should be taken as relating specifically to England and Wales only. Some comments on the legal professions in both Scotland and Northern Ireland are on pages 28, 44 and 58.

WHAT DO LAW GRADUATES DO?

At present there are almost 13,000 places on law and combined law degree courses in the UK; but with over 20,000 applications for those places, competition is still acute. After graduation law graduates go into a variety of areas. In 1996 over half went on to further study or training that included the professional legal training courses, the Legal Practice Course (LPC) and the Bar Vocational Course (BVC). Less than three in ten went straight into work, which included employment as diverse as officer training in the Army, newspaper journalism and marketing.

You will also find law graduates in banking, accountancy, management consultancy and the Civil Service. This shows that a law degree, even without further professional training, is a highly marketable degree and sought after by many employers.

Women in the legal profession

The number of women law graduates now exceeds the number of men. In 1997 there were 4876 female law graduates compared with 4016 of their male counterparts. However, this has not yet been translated into the profession. According to the Law Society in 1999 the number of women solicitors with practising certificates is approximately half the number of men: 25,439 female solicitors compared with 49,633 male solicitors.

The Bar Council presents a similar picture, with 2410 practising female barristers in England and Wales in 1998, compared with 7288 male. At the top of the profession the difference is even greater, with only 72 female QCs (Queen's Counsel) and 934 male QCs. But the situation seems to vary between different chambers.

One young, newly qualified female barrister said that women were well represented at her chambers but others were very male dominated. 'Equality still does not exist at the Bar,' she commented. 'It can be harder to get work of a certain quality. Tenacity is the key. Women need to be more flexible and take the opportunities when they come.' Yet at a firm of City solicitors a trainee noted that in her intake 10 out of 13 were women. So hopefully slow but steady progress into the 21st century...

Mature entrants to the legal profession

A good majority of solicitors qualify under the age of 30 and it is not common to qualify once over 40. The situation is the same at the Bar where the success of finding pupillage is greatly reduced for those over the age of 30. However, attitudes of firms and chambers vary considerably. But there is no doubt that if you are a mature candidate, say over 30, you will be at an advantage if you have previous relevant work experience and can demonstrate that you are good with clients. If you are older it is vital that you find out what it would be like to work in a firm of solicitors or chambers to 'test the water'.

On the other hand, it can still be useful to do something else after graduating before deciding on a career in the law. One newly qualified barrister said:

> *'After my English Literature degree I did one year's voluntary work abroad then joined the Civil Service Fast Stream for two*

years before training as a barrister. I think it is very important to go into something else beforehand. Quite a lot of barristers have done other things that can be useful, such as teaching.'

Developments to be aware of

The legal profession is constantly changing. So it is very important you keep up to date if you are thinking about a legal career. A good habit is reading the legal press such as the legal pages of the major newspapers (eg *The Times* on a Tuesday); also professional journals such as *The Law Society Gazette* and *The Lawyer*.

- Firms still place much emphasis on good A-level grades in their selection criteria.

- There is evidence that employers still look at the 'old' universities or what they perceive to be 'good' universities for their trainees. So in some cases students who had to study at regional universities because of financial constraints may be discriminated against.

- More and more students are completing their professional studies part time, mostly due to the lack of financial support.

- The number of students graduating from the LPC without training contracts is reducing, probably due to the fall in students applying for the LPC and the increase in available training contracts. In 1998 there were almost 5500 students on the full-time LPC, a drop of over 800 from 1997.

- The number of registered two-year training contracts has increased. In 1998 there were 4826 training contracts available, an increase of 100 on the previous year.

- For the 1998/99 BVC, 2667 applicants applied for 1430 full-time places available on the BVC.

- Growth of paralegals – more paralegals are being recruited to do routine work. But this is often seen as a way in for LPC and BVC students.

- Technology has overhauled communications by the introduction of email, voicemail, video conferencing as well as the advantages of the Internet.

- Solicitors' firms have become much more international.

WHAT WILL I STUDY ON A LAW DEGREE?

This section will give you a brief flavour of some of the issues you could study on a law degree, and provide you with some material for discussion if you are called for interview by a university law school.

Miscarriages of criminal justice

The term 'miscarriage of justice' is widely used, but seldom defined. The Royal Commission on Criminal Justice (1993) – the Runciman Commission – recognised that the term could incorporate the acquittal of the guilty as well as the conviction of the innocent, but it is miscarriages in the latter sense that have been the greatest concern in recent years. For many years it has hardly been possible to open a newspaper without being presented with revelations of yet another miscarriage of justice. What has been happening to the English criminal justice system?

You might want to consider what leads to wrongful conviction. Here are some prime causes to consider.

1. Mistakes of fact

These are the least controversial aspects of the problem. Wrongful convictions may arise where no one is truly at fault. This is because the conviction will appear correct on the evidence available at the time, but that evidence later proves to be incomplete or inaccurate. For example, where evidence supporting an accused's alibi only comes to light after the trial; or where flaws in the forensic evidence against an accused were not identifiable given the state of scientific knowledge at the time of trial.

There are some safeguards in the system that try to identify and prevent these errors, but there is obviously a limited capacity in any system of justice to stop such mistakes happening. Whether present safeguards are adequate is a point of debate. The Birmingham Six, the alleged IRA activists who were wrongly convicted of bombing two Birmingham pubs in 1974, had their case reviewed three times by the Court of Appeal before their convictions were finally quashed in 1991.

2. Procedural inequality

The defence lawyer Michael Mansfield QC has argued strongly that one of the problems of the English system is that the defence is placed at a disadvantage from the outset. For example, he argues that the defence lack the physical and financial resources of the state. Forensic evidence of the crime, for instance, is gathered and tested by Home Office forensic scientists. Although the results are made available to the defence, there is a general shortage of independent forensic services to allow the defence to carry out its own assessment.

3. Procedural impropriety

One of the greatest causes of concern is the extent to which misconviction is the result of deliberate or negligent behaviour by participants in the criminal justice system. Cases have disclosed impropriety by the police; by expert witnesses; by prosecution counsel and by the judge.

Most of these cases involve breaches of the rules governing the detention and questioning of suspects. Thus the conviction, in 1988, of Jacqueline Fletcher, a 28-year-old woman with a mental age of 10, who confessed to murdering her baby, was overturned in 1992 because of flagrant abuse of questioning procedures. Such examples suggest that some fairly fundamental problems still remain in policing practice. What is it about existing methods and procedures that encourage the police, at least in some cases, to find a suspect and then make sure that the evidence fits? Is the problem purely one of a few rogue officers? How do we stop these things happening?

There are no definitive answers to all the questions that these miscarriages of justice surely raise. The Runciman Commission was set up in 1991 to propose its own solutions. A number of these have been implemented, but are themselves the subject of continuing debate in both the academic and the national press.

The future of trial by jury

When you conjure up an image of a trial, an integral element will almost certainly be the jury. The principle of trial-by-jury is rooted in the medieval origins of English law, and it remains a powerful part of the ideology of law. In theory, everyone retains the right to 'trial by one's peers', and jury trial is widely represented as a safeguard against oppressive government or the conviction-minded judge. But what is the reality?

The process of jury trial

One of the greatest causes of concern is the extent to which misconviction is the result of deliberate or negligent behaviour by participants in the criminal justice system. Any citizen who is over 18 and under 65, who is not disqualified by virtue of some specific rule, may be required to do jury service. Juries are selected randomly on a local basis from the electoral register. If you are selected, you will be expected to attend your local Crown Court centre with other potential jurors. Each jury must consist of 12 persons.

It is the jury's decision whether or not a person is innocent or guilty on the evidence presented in court. The jury is advised as to the law by a professionally qualified judge, but the decision on the facts is theirs alone. The jury's decision, or 'verdict' is given at the end of the trial, in open court. It must normally be a unanimous one, though in exceptional circumstances the judge may accept a majority verdict. Where the result is a guilty verdict the sentence is determined by the judge, not the jury.

The basic principle in criminal cases is that a defendant will be tried by jury in relation to any offence that is triable in the Crown Court. This court has jurisdiction over a wide range of offences, including the most serious crimes, such as murder, manslaughter, rape and arson, but also many lesser offences against the person or property. Even so, on average, less than 10% of all criminal trials are heard before the Crown Court, with the remainder being dealt with by Justices of the Peace in the Magistrates' Court.

WHAT IF I DON'T WANT TO GO INTO LAW AFTER MY DEGREE?

Some students study law with no intention of becoming a professional lawyer. The legal knowledge and additional skills gained from a law degree is highly prized and can be applied to a number of jobs. We will look at those skills in more detail in Chapters 4 and 5.

But what else can a law graduate do other than practise law? If you use Clive Anderson or Bill Clinton as your role models the world is your oyster, but here are a few suggestions as to what the rest do...

- **Accountancy**
  Many aspects of accountancy relate to those found in legal practice such as analysing large amounts of technical material, analysing and writing reports and advising clients. Law graduates are often particularly wooed into tax consultancy. Starting salaries are usually high.

- **Administration**
  You need a methodical and precise approach as well as good written and communication skills for this job. Some administrative work is in private industry but most jobs are found in the Civil Service, local government, the health service, voluntary organisations and further and higher education institutions.

- **Civil Service**
  Interested in policy making and implementation? Then you might

think about Civil Service departments with legal responsibilities such as the Home Office, Inland Revenue, Lord Chancellor's Department and Foreign Office. The Customs and Excise Office and Immigration Service would also value law graduates.

- **Business management**
  The skills you developed from a law degree will be invaluable in the world of commerce and industry.

- **The City and finance**
  A number of law graduates are lured into the highly paid world of investment banking and insurance where your legal background will give you an edge. But beware that competition is extremely tough for these jobs with high rewards.

In addition to the above areas law graduates also go into legal publishing, the media, journalism (legal or otherwise), the police service, teaching, personnel and a lot more...

Some law graduates choose not to pursue the training to become either a solicitor or a barrister but would still like to do something legally related. They will often move into fields such as paralegal and outdoor clerk work. Paralegals research cases, scan and collate documents, whereas outdoor clerks take witness statements on behalf of solicitors' clients and conduct legal research for solicitors, barristers and others, and do any administrative work that is required.

Chapter 2
WHAT DO SOLICITORS DO?

WHAT'S THE WORK LIKE?

Solicitors usually work in firms. Some work for large companies as part of their in-house legal departments (eg the trademarks division) but most are in private practice. In 1999 there were 60,818 solicitors in private practice compared with only 4661 in commerce and industry. Firms vary in size from two people to hundreds, employing assistant solicitors and trainees as well as the actual partners. The larger the firm the more specialised the individual solicitor's work will be. A small firm in your local high street may undertake a wide range of activities such as drafting wills, conveying houses, dealing with divorces and sorting out landlord and tenant issues.

Larger firms have specialist departments like a commercial litigation department, or one covering employment, shipping law or tax. The list of legal specialisms is extensive. *The Chambers and Partners Guide to the Legal Profession* lists them. But the depth of expertise required can sometimes mean that even large firms only deal with a narrow range of topics.

The main work of solicitors is to act as the first port of call for a client needing help in organising their affairs or as a potential litigant (plaintiff or defendant). If the client needs a will drafting, for instance, the solicitor will interview the client, take all relevant details and advise on the legal implications of a particular course of action. The solicitor would then draft the will or other document and, once all the points have been explained to the client, ensure that all the formalities are completed.

If the client is involved in a dispute the solicitor will often try to resolve the matter by writing to the other party. If the dispute continues the solicitor will then advise on litigation. (But the best advice is to avoid litigation at all costs!) Their work will then involve taking statements, collecting evidence and preparing the case for trial. In some instances where the amount involved is small the solicitor may represent the client in court. If the client needs help on a criminal law point the solicitor will have to gather the evidence, which may involve a visit to the police station or prison where the client is in custody in order to take instructions.

A solicitor's work can be extremely varied and has the advantage of direct contact with many different types of people. On the other hand, a number of solicitors complain that they deal less with legal points and more with matters like interviewing, counselling, paperwork and office management.

WHAT MAKES A GOOD SOLICITOR?

Solicitors need a vast range of qualities to make them effective (see Chapter 4 for more details on specific skills). But it is commonly recognised that to get a job you need something to make you stand out from the crowd. Some language and computer skills as well as being outgoing and demonstrating a sense of humour will give you the edge. You will also need to be someone who is focused and persistent and who can provide plenty of evidence of working well with others in a team.

CASE STUDY

Working in a large City firm

Sukhraj is a Senior Associate Solicitor with Allen & Overy, a large firm of City solicitors, and has worked for them for over seven years. She went to university in Leicester straight after A-levels and gained an upper second class law degree before taking her professional training at the College of Law in Chester. 'The training contract was not too much of a culture shock after being a student. There were 60 trainees and it was just like going into a smaller class and not nearly as bad as I thought it would be!' commented Sukhraj. 'We were given loads of training and everyone was very friendly.' During her training she experienced four seats, which are in effect placements in different departments. This included six months in New York in the Banking Department. She confirmed there are now lots of seats abroad although most are still very sought after.

She now works in the Projects Department, involving her in project finance plus a lot of banking and international work. 'You need to be willing to take responsibility and be a team player,' says Sukhraj, 'but you also need to be able to work on your own.' Her training is ongoing as the Law Society stipulates that all

solicitors must do at least 16 hours per year to accumulate continuing education points. Training can take the form of lunchtime lectures, full-day courses and residential courses. Sukhraj advises that if you are interested in working for a big City firm it is essential you become familiar with the City. 'It's very important to read the quality papers and you need to acquire some commercial know-how,' she says. A summer placement is the best way of getting experience. Her hours vary considerably depending what she is working on, but 9am until 7pm is average. 'Working late into the night is very common,' she adds.

Working in a provincial firm

Martin is in the second year of his training contract with a firm of solicitors in Brighton. His first degree is in French and he then went on to complete the Common Professional Examination (CPE) and the Legal Practice Course before starting his training contract. He studied for his degree in London and says he finds it a refreshing change to be out of the big city but still somewhere where there is a lot going on. 'I enjoyed the LPC,' says Martin, 'It was very practical and really tried to teach you the skills needed to do the job. But

nothing can totally prepare you for what it's really like.'

Martin's first few weeks were spent getting used to all the office systems before he started on a formalised training programme covering the two years of his training contract. During that period he will spend time in four seats. 'Trainees have access at all times to a partner or senior solicitor who can help out with any difficulties if required. I'm really enjoying the work and find myself becoming more and more confident all the time.'

Working as an in-house lawyer

Katrina works as an in-house lawyer for an American film production company based in London. She's been there for over four years, starting as a manager, and is now Director of International Legal and Business Affairs. She was offered the job when working as an entertainment lawyer with a firm of solicitors who specialise in media and entertainment law.

'When I moved to my present company it was an enormous transition from my previous firm,' says Katrina. 'I suddenly found myself working with a lot of creative people including producers instead of mainly with lawyers. Here I am very much part of the production team and there are no time sheets to complete, unlike a firm of solicitors!' The actual work she does is very similar, such as arranging production contracts, but the atmosphere is totally different. 'Here I am now the only lawyer although I have a contracts manager and secretary.'

Because she is the only lawyer in her office she admits she also gets a lot of the 'rubbish jobs' which she shouldn't be doing. Many other in-house lawyers would have a legal executive to do this work.

Katrina comments that American companies seem to be more keen on having in-house lawyers than do UK ones. She says you need to be a person who is fairly independent and willing to take total responsibility. Her advice to anyone wanting to work in-house is to train in private practice first. She comments that working in-house is often not as good financially as working in a firm but certainly in her field she believes that those interested in media law want to work in the industry rather than just being a lawyer. 'It's also an excellent way of making contacts – which is so very important.' She reckons it is advisable to work at least one year after qualifying before going in-house.

WHO WORKS WHERE?

The vast majority of solicitors work in private practice in a firm of solicitors. But qualified solicitors have a huge choice of organisations in which they could work potentially. The legal profession truly does cater for everyone... from those wishing to specialise in a huge international City-based firm to those preferring to do a 'bit of everything' in a small high street firm.

According to the Law Society, the 75,072 qualified solicitors are working in the following areas:

Where solicitors work	Number
Private practice	60,818
Commerce & industry	4,661
Accountancy practice	67
Nationalised industry	78
Trade union	48
Government department	49
Local government	2,845
Court	165
Government-funded services	142
Crown Prosecution Service	1,525
Advice service	273
Educational establishment	107
Health Service	24
Others	1,100
Practising certificate holders not attached to an organisation	3,170

What if I want to work abroad?

Prospects for lawyers wishing to pursue an international career and work abroad have grown greatly in recent years. Opportunities exist to work in the offices of partner firms in other countries, work in the legal department of an international client or even work abroad as part of your training contract. Some big firms have an established international network worldwide. Other opportunities are being created by the increase in overseas firms opening offices in the UK. 'Training with a big international firm gives you so much opportunity for working abroad and travelling,' says one trainee. There are more and more opportunities for lawyers with international experience. If you have spent some time working abroad as a lawyer it is bound to be an asset to future career prospects. The European Commission also recruits qualified lawyers through open competition but does not recruit trainees. Opportunities for international work at the Bar are very limited.

Chapter 3
WHAT DO BARRISTERS DO?

WHAT'S THE WORK LIKE?

One of the complaints about the English legal system is that lawyers are like buses: as soon as one appears a whole string of them arrives. This impression comes from the fact that solicitors may often employ barristers to give specialist advice or to represent the client in court. So, instead of hiring only one lawyer, you now have at least two on your hands.

We said earlier that the work of barristers compares with consultants or surgeons; they are specialist advocates. Barristers work as individuals and cannot form partnerships with other lawyers. They do form loose groups called 'chambers' where a small number will have their offices in the same building and share the expenses of clerks and common facilities, but these are not firms. Barristers are responsible for their own caseloads.

Barristers also come in two forms: junior counsel and senior counsel. This has nothing to do with age, but indicates generally whether a barrister has 'taken silk' or not. This odd phrase relates to the silk used in the gowns worn by senior barristers and it means that the barrister has been appointed 'Queen's Counsel' (QC). A QC is therefore a senior barrister, appearing only in the more important cases in the higher courts, and charging very much higher senior fees.

A solicitor might want to employ a barrister for two main reasons. First, to gain another opinion on a matter of law from a person who is particularly authoritative in that field of law. Second, to represent the client in court where the solicitor is not allowed to or would prefer a specialist advocate to take on the task. When a solicitor asks for a barrister's view on a legal point this is known as seeking 'counsel's opinion'. Where the barrister is asked to undertake litigation work, this is known as 'instructing counsel'. If an opinion is sought the barrister will be sent all the relevant paperwork and will sit down and research that area of law before expressing a view as to the merits of the case.

If counsel is instructed to act then, generally speaking, the decision to litigate or defend will have been taken and the barrister will begin to prepare his or her arguments, which they will later argue in court. So most of the barrister's work will be centred on legal disputes. The barrister acts like the old medieval champion: stepping in to fight in the place of the client.

There are over 9000 barristers in independent practice in England and Wales. They specialise in a wide variety of areas including Building and Construction, Commercial Company, Criminal, Employment, Personal Injury, Liquidation, Taxation, Property and many more. Barristers also work for the Crown Prosecution Service (CPS), the Government Legal Service (GLS) and the Inner London Magistrates Courts.

Barristers' work usually comes through the referral of a solicitor. Sometimes, barristers provide their services 'pro bono' such as through the Free Representation Units or the Bar Pro Bono Unit. In some humanitarian cases pro bono work has also been carried out.

There has recently been a great increase in the size of the Bar. This has meant that the number of chambers has also increased. Most barristers practise from London but nearly 3000 barristers practise from other large cities in the UK as well as some small towns outside London.

WHO WORKS WHERE?

According to the Bar Council the numbers of barristers working in the following areas are:

Where barristers work	Number
Independent Bar	9369
Crown Prosecution Service	579
Government Legal Service	386
Inner London Magistrates Courts	72
Magistrates & Justices Clerks	320
Other employed barristers	1059

WHAT MAKES A GOOD BARRISTER?

'You need to have utter confidence in what you are doing – or at least appear to,' says one newly qualified young barrister. 'You are absolutely vulnerable to the whims of the solicitor. You put your soul into a piece of work and you need to be robust so as not to take it too personally.'

Vital to the barrister's work is the ability to persuade, so strong communication skills are at the top of the list. To be an effective barrister you also need to be interested in business and be commercially aware. See Chapter 5 for more detail on the skills required.

CASE STUDY

The experienced barrister

Paul is an experienced barrister who has been working from chambers in London since 1985. Most of his work is with insurers, giving them advice on whether or not they should meet a claim. He deals a lot with recovery work and employers' liability.

'It is very important to build up your reputation. This often starts with your clerk who will recommend you to do a piece of work from solicitors. After that you'll tend to build up your reputation by word of mouth,' says Paul. 'Your task in court is to persuade the tribunal, so good communication skills are vitally important. You also need to communicate effectively with your own clients. A good grasp of the law and the enthusiasm to carry on learning is necessary.' A lot of stamina is required to be a barrister as the job is very hard work, often requiring you to work more than 10-hour days, sometimes six or seven days a week. 'Working from 6am until midnight is common, especially on a long case which can go on for weeks on end,' he says.

Because it is a tough profession Paul advises that you should give it serious thought. 'It's also a very enjoyable profession. For people who like to be independent and work for themselves – it's the ideal profession. But you need to be able to work on your own initiative and find a way of managing the workload and your free time so that it doesn't entirely dominate your life,' he comments.

And qualifications? Paul advises: 'You will require a minimum 2:1 degree and you should do a mini-pupillage, preferably at places you plan to apply to for pupillage.'

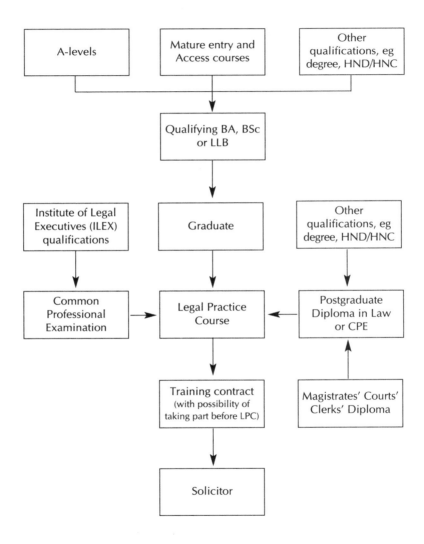

Main routes to qualifying as a solicitor

MAIN ROUTES TO QUALIFYING AS A SOLICITOR

There are a number of routes into the legal profession as you can see from the diagram on the previous page.

A-levels and equivalents

Nearly all A-level subjects are acceptable. Legal study is something of a cross between the arts and sciences, so a combination of subjects would be a very good grounding. Contrary to popular belief, taking law at A-level is not an advantage for a law degree. It is also quite common for General Studies to be discounted by some universities. You'll need to pay particular attention to each law school's entrance requirements. Also note that an A-level modern language could be an advantage if you apply for a job with one of the big law firms.

But you will need to have a strong academic background. University admissions tutors and subsequently firms of solicitors will look for three good A-level grades (or their equivalent) as part of their selection criteria. Specific grades will vary but the 'old' universities and the big firms will certainly look for and get candidates with mostly grades A and B.

Access courses

A-levels need not be the only entry pathway. Many universities encourage mature students (who may have missed out on the opportunity to enter higher education) to apply for entry on to degree courses, taking into account their work experience and commitment as part of the entry criteria. Access courses in colleges around the country specifically prepare mature students for higher education.

Mature students now constitute a third of the intake in many university law faculties. The difficulties they face are that they are not as accustomed to study as the young A-level entrant, but they possess an advantage in that law is concerned with the everyday practical problems that they may well have faced.

The law degree

There are many variations in the design of law degrees. You will find courses concentrating on traditional law subjects, or ones involving a high percentage of European or comparative law, or joint degrees (eg Law and Politics). You must choose one that suits your interests and possible career path. But if you are going to pursue a career as a solicitor you will need to ensure that the degree is a 'qualifying degree'. This is one recognised by the Law Society, as containing the subjects you must study for your degree. Most LLB (Bachelor of Law) courses will be qualifying degrees but you need to check first. Contact the Law Society for a list of qualifying law degrees (and see the table starting on page 29).

Many courses offer you the choice of optional subjects that allow some specialism within your course. These options may even extend to non-law subjects such as forensic science or accounts.

During a normal three-year course students would expect at least 50% of their workload to be studying law. The seven foundation subjects on a law degree are: contract, tort, equity and trusts, criminal law, property law, public law and European Union law. It is important to gain a minimum 2:1 degree, as it is very difficult to get a training contract with a lower degree.

The non-law degree

You can go on to qualify as a solicitor with a degree from any discipline. Following this route you will have to complete the Common Professional Examination (CPE) or its equivalent – the Postgraduate Diploma in Law (PGDL). Both courses are one year full time or two years part time.

The CPE/Diploma in Law

If you take a degree subject other than law you can still pursue a legal career. But you will need to take a course that concentrates on the fundamental principles required by the Law Society (the same subjects that are demanded in a qualifying law degree. Courses known as the Common Professional Examination or a Postgraduate Diploma in Law are offered by a number of universities. Both courses are intensive and usually last one academic year full time or two years part time. (See the table on page 38.)

The Legal Practice Course

The LPC is the professional stage of training for prospective solicitors. Most LPC courses have a commercial bias and are very intensive and hard work. The first-time average national pass rate is just under 70%. There are around 30 institutions validated by the Law Society to provide the LPC. On every LPC course six skills areas are taught. These are: practical legal research; writing and drafting; interviewing and advising; and advocacy. There are also three main compulsory subjects, business law and practice, conveyancing and litigation. Assessment is normally a combination of examination and coursework. In 1997/98 there were many more places available on the LPC than were filled by students.

A student who has passed the Legal Practice Course cannot yet be called a solicitor. To gain this title you will need to undertake a 'training contract', usually taken in a firm of solicitors. The training contract will last two years. During that time you will be instructed in various aspects of legal work, spending time in each department within the firm. The crunch comes after the LPC when potential lawyers fight for positions as trainee solicitors. Competition still exists to secure a training contract so although you might get on to an LPC with a lower second class degree or less your chances of getting a training contract will be greatly reduced. (See the table on page 38 for a list of LPC providers.

Legal Practice Course student

Mark was always very clear about his career aspirations, but decided that to have the option of specialising in intellectual property he needed to complete a science degree as some of the work can involve patents and scientific know-how. He studied Chemistry at Imperial College and spent two years in London and two in Paris, where he did research and studied French literature. Mark then applied to do his CPE at the College of Law in London.

'I wanted to move back to London after Paris and wanted to be at the college, because it has a reputation for quality courses and is well recognised by leading firms. I had already started doing vacation placements at various firms and knew that although I enjoyed the research, long term I wanted to work in a more people-oriented profession.'

Mark found the CPE very fast paced and practical, which is excellent for a scientist who has always dealt with the practical applications of his experiments. 'CPE students do miss out a little on discussing the implications of law, but the practical aspects are great and really prepare you for life in a law firm.'

Mark had always been part of a debating team, all through school and university, and when he arrived at the college he was keen to help give the debating team a boost. 'Debating introduces you to the skills of presenting your case logically and in public. All solicitors will need these skills as they have to be able to talk to clients, think on their feet and justify their actions in an ordered and coherent way.'

FUNDING

Gaining a professional qualification takes time and costs a lot of money. At the time of writing, fees alone for the LPC are at least £6000 at most institutions, notwithstanding the costs for accommodation and subsistence.

You may be able to secure financial assistance for your professional training from one or more of the following sources:

■ Local authority grants – Contact your local education authority for information.

■ Bank loans – A number of banks offer loans at favourable rates.

- Career Development Loans – These are operated on behalf of the Department for Education and Employment by a number of high street banks. For a free booklet on Career Development Loans phone 0800 585 505.

- Charities and Grant-Making Trusts – Refer to the books *The Charities Digest* and *The Directory of Grant-Making Trusts*.

- Law Society Bursary Scheme – Contact the Law Society for information.

- College Access funds – Contact Student Services at each university for information.

- Ethnic minority students – Contact the Law Society for information on a limited number of scholarships available.

SKILLS AND QUALITIES

The key skills and qualities you will need as a solicitor are:

- Strong academic background
- Good written and verbal communication skills
- Commercial awareness
- Interpersonal skills
- Ability to work under pressure
- Computer skills
- Numeracy
- Time management skills
- Attention to detail
- Ability to take personal responsibility

...and many more.

Working as a Trainee Solicitor

Carole completed her LLB degree in English and French Law at the University of Kent before studying for her LPC at the College of Law in Guildford. 'Studying legal French was very hard,' says Carole 'but it helped me to stand out from the crowd when applying for jobs.' She eventually succeeded in securing her training contract with a large firm of City solicitors while in her final year. Part of the selection process involved her presenting to two partners on a miscarriage of justice.

Carole started her training contract in 1998. Her first seat was in the Corporate Department. 'Work was extremely hectic but it was an excellent way for me to get integrated. I have been involved in some major transactions including one worth eight million dollars. Part of my job was to coordinate teams of international lawyers so I had to use my organising skills, and also my French language skills were useful.

'The Corporate Department is all or nothing,' says Carole. 'It's either very quiet or when you are working on a transaction you can be working round the clock.' Other departments such as Property and Employment have more regular hours. 'I now have the option of going to Brussels for three months and after I've qualified I can go anywhere in the world.'

The firm Carole works for is huge worldwide but the London office is only medium sized. 'This is great as you get to know everyone really well,' says Carole. 'There's a good induction programme and a comprehensive system of support so there is always someone to help you when you need it.' However, because of the intense competition for training contracts Carole thinks you really need something to help you stand out. 'Being outgoing, having a sense of humour, language and computer skills will give you the edge,' she says. 'I also had quite a lot of legal experience which is very important.'

She advises: 'You must be very committed before going to law school as costs are great unless you are sponsored. Be focused and persistent.' Carole says her firm has a good attitude to women. Out of her group of trainees there were ten women and three men. 'As a trainee I started on £21,000pa. I've been given lots of responsibility and the chance to get involved.'

QUALIFYING AS A SOLICITOR IN SCOTLAND

The legal system in Scotland differs from that of England and Wales and Northern Ireland. It is not possible to go into great detail in this book, but here is a summary.

A Bachelor of Law degree (LLB) is offered at five Scottish universities as an ordinary degree over three years or an Honours degree over four years. Admission requirements to all LLB degrees are high. After completion of the LLB degree all intending solicitors are required to take the Diploma in Legal Practice, which lasts seven months. The course has been designed to teach the practical knowledge and skills necessary for the working life of a solicitor. After successful completion of the degree and diploma, you need to serve a two-year post-diploma training contract with a practising solicitor in Scotland. For further information contact The Law Society of Scotland. (See Chapter 11 for address; also page 59.)

QUALIFYING AS A SOLICITOR IN NORTHERN IRELAND

Again, it is not possible to go into detail, but here is a summary: law graduates who wish to practise in Northern Ireland should apply for the one-year Vocational Certificate course at Queen's University, Belfast. Non-law graduates must complete the two-year Bachelor of Legal Science Studies at the same university before taking the Vocational Certificate course. For further information contact The Law Society of Northern Ireland. (See Chapter 11 for address; also page 52.)

QUALIFYING LAW DEGREES FOR ENGLAND AND WALES

The following table lists the institutions in England and Wales offering full-time law degrees, giving the qualification gained and title of the degree. It is essential that you check the current prospectuses for full details of courses to which you plan to apply.

Universities (full time)	Degree Awarded	Title of Degree
Aberystwyth	LLB	Law
(University College of Wales)	LLB	Law & European Language
01970 623 111	BSc (Econ)	Law & Economics
	BSc (Econ)	Law & Political Science
	BSc (Econ)	Law & Accounting & Finance
	BSc (Econ)	Law & Business Studies
	BA	Law
	BA	Law with European Languages
Anglia Polytechnic	LLB	Law
University	BA	Combined Honours
01245 493131		
Aston University	BSc	Managerial & Admin Studies
0121 359 3611		
University of Central	LLB	Law (including language options)
England	LLB	Law with Politics
0121 331 5000	BA	Law & Minor Studies
Birmingham University	LLB	Law
0121 414 3344	LLB	Law with French
	LLB	Law & Business Studies
	LLB	Law & Politics
	LLB	Law & European Law
Bournemouth University	LLB	Business Law (sandwich)
01202 524111	LLB	Law
	LLB	Law & Taxation
Bradford & Ilkley College	LLB	Law
01274 753111		
University of the West of	LLB	Law
England in Bristol	LLB	European Law & Languages
0117 965 6261	LLB	Law & Comparative European Legal Studies
Bristol University	LLB	Law
0117 928 7453	LLB	Law & French
	LLB	Law & German
	LLB	European Legal Studies
	BSc	Chemistry & Law

29

Universities (full time)	Degree Awarded	Title of Degree
University of Brighton 01273 642570	BA	Law & Accountancy
Brunel University 01895 274000	LLB LLB LLB BSc BSc	Business & Finance Law Law French/German Economics & Law (incl sandwich) Management Studies & Law
Buckingham University 01280 814080	LLB LLB LLB LLB	Law (2 years duration) European Studies (2 years) Law, Biology & Environment (2 years) Politics & Law (2 years)
Cambridge University 01223 337733	BA	Law Tripos
Cardiff (University of Wales) 01222 382656	LLB LLB LLB LLB LLB LLB LLB LLB	Law Law & French Law & German Law & Italian Law & Japanese Law & Spanish Law & Sociology Law & Politics
Coventry University 01203 631313	LLB LLB LLB LLB	Legal Studies Business Law Criminal Justice with English European Law with a Language
De Montfort University 01162 551 551	LLB LLB LLB BA BSc	Law Law with French Law with German Combined Studies Combined Studies
University of Derby 01332 622222	LLB	Law
Dundee University 01382 344461	LLB LLB LLB LLB	English Law Law & Accountancy Law with French Law with German (in all cases the courses on the English Law stream must be taken)

Universities (full time)	Degree Awarded	Title of Degree
Durham University	LLB	Law
0191 374 2000	BA	Law & Economics
	BA	Law & Politics
	BA	Law & Sociology
	LLB	European Legal Studies
East Anglia University	LLB	Law
01603 56161	LLB	Law with German Law & Language
	LLB	Law with French Law & Language
	LLB	Law with European Legal Systems
Essex University	LLB	Law
01206 873333	LLB	English & European Law
	LLB	European Law with Sociology
	LLB	English & French Law
Exeter University	LLB	Law
01392 263263	LLB	European Law
	BA (Law)	Law & Society
	BA (Law)	Chemistry & Law
University of Glamorgan	LLB	Law
01443 480480		
University of Hertfordshire	LLB	Law
01707 284000	LLB	Law (2 years)
	BSc	Combined Studies
	BA	Social Science
	BA	Business Studies (Law major)
University of Huddersfield	LLB	Law
01484 422288	LLB	Business Law
	BA	Law & Accountancy
Hull University	LLB	Law
01482 46311	LLB	Law with French
	LLB	Law with German
University of Humberside & Lincolnshire 01482 440550	BA	Law & another subject
Keele University 01782 621111	BA	Law & another subject

Universities (full time)	Degree Awarded	Title of Degree
Kent University	LLB	Law
01227 764000	LLB	English & French Law
	LLB	English & German Law
	LLB	English & Italian Law
	LLB	English & Spanish Law
	LLB	European Legal Studies
	BA	Combined Studies
Kingston University	LLB	Law
0181 547 2000	BA	Accounting & Law
	LLB	Law with French
	LLB	Law with German
University of Central	LLB	Law
Lancashire	LLB	Law & French
01772 201201	LLB	Law & German
	BA	Law (Combined Honours)
	BSc	Law (Combined Honours)
Lancaster University	LLB	Law
01524 65201	LLB	European Legal Studies
Leeds Metropolitan University	LLB	Law
0113 283 2600	BA	Law with IT
Leeds University	LLB	Law
0113 243 1751	LLB	English Law with French/German Law
	LLB	Law & Chinese Studies
	LLB	Law & Japanese Studies
	LLB	Law & French Studies
Leicester University	LLB	Law
0116 222 522	LLB	Law with French
	LLB	Law with European Studies
	BA	Law & Economics
Liverpool John Moores University 0151 231 2121	LLB	Law
Liverpool University	LLB	Law
0151 794 2000	LLB	Law & French
	LLB	Law & German
	LLB	Law & Accounting
	LLB	Law & Economics

Universities (full time)	Degree Awarded	Title of Degree
UNIVERSITY OF LONDON		
London School of Economics	LLB	Law
& Political Science	LLB	Law with German
0171 955 7007	LLB	Law with French
	LLB	Law & Anthropology
	LLB	Law & Government
King's College	LLB	Law
0171 580 1122	LLB	English & French Law
	LLB	Law with German Law
School of Oriental &	LLB	Law
African Studies	BA	Law & another discipline
0171 637 2388	BA	Law & a language
Queen Mary & Westfield	LLB	Law
College	LLB	English & European Law
0171 975 5555	LLB	Law with German Language
	BA	Law & Economics
	BA	Law & Politics
	BA	Law & German
University College	LLB	Law
0171 387 7050	LLB	Law with Advanced Studies
	LLB	Law with French Law
	LLB	Law with German Law
	LLB	Law with Italian Law
	BA	Law & History
OTHER UNIVERSITIES IN LONDON		
City University	LLB	Law
0171 477 8000	LLB	Business Law
University of East London	LLB	Law
0181 590 7722	BA	Law (major)
University of Greenwich	LLB	Law
0181 316 8000	BA	Law
London Guildhall	LLB	Law
University	LLB	Business Law
0171 320 1000	BA	Legal Studies
	BA	Law & another discipline
Middlesex University	LLB	Law
0181 362 5000	BA	Law (major)

Universities (full time)	Degree Awarded	Title of Degree
University of North London 0171 607 2789	LLB	Law
South Bank University 0171 928 8989	LLB	Law
Thames Valley University 0181 579 5000	LLB	Law
	LLB	Law with French Law & Language
	LLB	Law with German Law & Language
	LLB	Law with Spanish Law & Language
	LLB	Law in the Community
	BA	Accounting & Law
	BA	European Law
	BA	Criminal Justice
University of Westminster 0171 911 5000	LLB	Law
	LLB	European Legal Studies
	BA	Law & Languages
University of Luton 01582 34111	LLB	Law
	BA	Law (major)
Manchester Metropolitan University 0161 247 2000	LLB	Law
	LLB	Law with French
	LLB	Law with German
Manchester University 0161 275 2000	LLB	Law
	LLB	English & French Law
	BA	Accounting & Law
	BA	Government & Law
Mid Kent College 01634 830633	BA	Law & Business Studies
	BA	Law & European Studies
	BA	Law & Politics
	BA	Law & Psychology
	BA	Law & Social Science
Newcastle upon Tyne University 0191 222 6000	LLB	Law
	BA	Accounting & Law
	BA	Law with French
Northampton: Nene College 01604 735500	LLB	Law
	LLB	Law & Languages

Universities (full time)	Degree Awarded	Title of Degree
University of Northumbria at Newcastle 0191 232 6002	LLB LLB	Law French & English Law
Nottingham Trent University 0115 941 8418	LLB LLB LLB	Law Law (sandwich) Magisterial Law
Nottingham University 0115 951 5151	LLB BA BA LLB/BA LLB/BA BA BA	Law Law Law & Politics Law with American Law Law with European Law Law with American Studies & Politics Law with European Law & Politics
Oxford Brookes University 01865 741111	LLB BA	Law Law & another subject
Oxford University 01865 270000	BA	Jurisprudence
University of Plymouth 01752 600600	LLB	Law
Queen's University, Belfast 01232 335081	LLB LLB LLB	Law Law & Accounting Common & Civil Law with French
Reading University 01734 875123	LLB LLB LLB	Law Law with French Law Law with Legal Studies in Europe
Sheffield Hallam University 0114 272 0911	LLB LLB LLB	Law Law (Canada) Law (Maîtresse en droit)
Sheffield University 0114 276 8555	LLB BA BA BA BA BA	Law Law Law & Criminology Law with French Law with German Law with Spanish

Universities (full time)	Degree Awarded	Title of Degree
Southampton Institute of Higher Education 01703 319000	LLB BA	Law Business & Law
Southampton University 01703 595000	LLB BSc BSc	Law Accounting & Law Politics & Law
Staffordshire University 01782 294550	LLB LLB LLB BA BA	Law Law & Language Law & Accounting Modern Studies Law & Another Subject
Surrey University 01483 300800	BSc BSc BSc	French & Law German & Law Russian & Law
Sussex University 01273 606755	LLB LLB LLB/BA BA BA BA	Law European Commercial Law Law with French Law/German Law/Italian Law/Spanish Law/ Russian Law Law with North American Studies Law with Economics Law with History
Swansea Institute of Higher Education 01792 481000	LLB	Law
University of Wales, Swansea 01792 481000	LLB LLB	Law Law with Business Studies, Language & Politics
University of Teesside 01642 218121	LLB	Law
Warwick University 01203 523523	LLB LLB BA BA	Law European Law Law & Sociology Law & Business
University of Wolverhampton 01902 321000	LLB BA	Law Law (Major)

Universities (full time)	Degree Awarded	Title of Degree
EIRE		
Trinity College, Dublin 00 3531 6772941	LLB	Law
University College, Cork 00 353 21 902 532	BCL BCL	Law French /German
University College, Dublin 00 3531 7067777	BCL	Law
University College, Galway 00 353 91 524411	LLB	Law
University of Limerick 00 353 61 202344	LLB	Law
University of Ulster 01265 44141	BA BA	Government & Law Law & Economics

INSTITUTIONS PROVIDING CPE/PGDL/LPC COURSES

The College of Law (London, Guildford, Chester & York)	CPE/PGDL, LPC
Anglia Polytechnic University	CPE/PGDL, LPC
University of Central England in Birmingham	CPE/PGDL, LPC
University of Birmingham	CPE/PGDL
Bournemouth University	CPE/PGDL, LPC
BPP Law School	CPE/PGDL, LPC
Cardiff University, Law School	LPC
University of Central Lancashire	CPE/PGDL, LPC
City University	CPE/PGDL
De Montfort University	CPE/PGDL, LPC
University of East Anglia	CPE/PGDL
University of Exeter	CPE/PGDL
University of Glamorgan	CPE/PGDL, LPC
University of Hertfordshire	LPC
Holborn College	CPE/PGDL
University of Huddersfield	CPE/PGDL, LPC
University of Keele	CPE/PGDL
Kingston University	CPE/PGDL
Leeds Metropolitan University	CPE/PGDL, LPC
Liverpool John Moores University	LPC
London Guildhall University	CPE/PGDL, LPC
Manchester Metropolitan University	CPE/PGDL, LPC
Middlesex University	CPE/PGDL
University of North London	CPE/PGDL, LPC
University of Northumbria at Newcastle	CPE/PGDL, LPC
Nottingham Trent University	CPE/PGDL, LPC
Oxford Brookes University	CPE/PGDL
Oxford Institute of Legal Practice	LPC
University of Sheffield	LPC
South Bank University	CPE/PGDL, LPC
Staffordshire University	CPE/PGDL, LPC
University of Sussex	CPE/PGDL
Thames Valley University	CPE/PGDL, LPC
University of Westminster	CPE/PGDL, LPC
University of the West of England	CPE/PGDL, LPC
Wolsey Hall College	CPE/PGDL
University of Wolverhampton	CPE/PGDL, LPC
Worcester College of Technology	CPE/PGDL

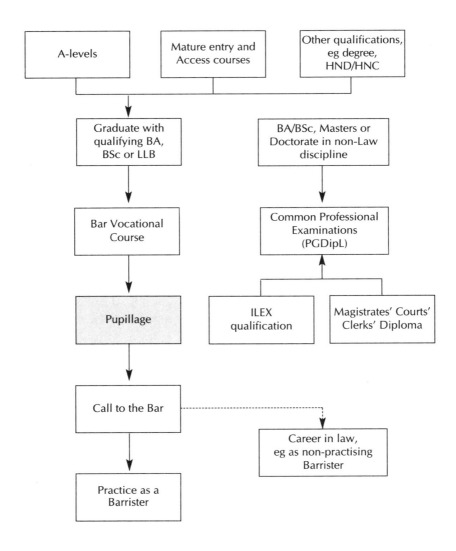

Main routes to qualifying as a barrister

MAIN ROUTES TO QUALIFYING AS A BARRISTER

A-levels and equivalents

Nearly all A-level subjects are acceptable. But it is most important to achieve excellent grades, preferably grades A and B, to stand a good chance of getting into a well-respected university and course. (See pages 29–37 for list of qualifying law degrees.

Access courses

Many universities encourage mature students to apply for entry. Some of these mature students will have attended an Access Course that has prepared them for higher education and further study. Previous relevant experience can sometimes put such applicants at an advantage.

The law degree

If you wish to qualify as a barrister you must be a graduate. Most, but not all, barristers will have studied a law degree (LLB). There are numerous varieties of law degrees. Some concentrate on traditional law subjects, while others include a variety of options. It is important to make sure that it is a qualifying law degree. You can do this by checking with the General Council of the Bar. (See Chapter 11 for the address.) You should aim for at least an upper second class degree as you will find it more difficult to obtain pupillage with a lower second or below.

The non-law degree

A significant number of barristers hold a degree in another subject other than law. Again it is very important to obtain a good class of degree, ideally an upper second or above.

The CPE/Diploma in Law

Graduates who have not obtained a law degree need to take an extra qualification in law. This is either the Common Professional Examination (CPE) or the Diploma in Law. Both courses normally last one year full time or two years part time. See page 38 for a list of providers.

The Bar Vocational Course (BVC)

To become a barrister entitled to practise the Bar Council requires you to take the one-year Bar Vocational Course (BVC). But before starting the BVC you will need to join one of the four Inns of Court. The BVC aims to help you gain the skills of advocacy, conference skills, drafting, fact management, legal research, negotiation and opinion writing to prepare you for the practical stage of training on the job, which is one year of pupillage. Pupillage involves observing a senior barrister (your 'pupil' master) at work for six months (unpaid) followed by a further period of six months where you may appear in court under the loose supervision of your pupil master. You are then on your own, to make as much or as little as your luck and skill allow.

Those wanting to become barristers are in for a tough time. Competition for places is keen. In 1998/99 there were 2667 applications for 1430 full-time places and 100 part-time places. The BVC is available at eight different teaching institutions throughout the country (see page 45). Prior to 1998 the Inns of Court School of Law was the only provider. On completion of the BVC a large proportion of people will be unable to get 'pupillage' but may be able to work for a legal department in a major company.

Bar Vocational Course Student

Kim ran her own prosperous car-spraying business for five years before deciding to embark on the long and uncertain route to the Bar. She successfully completed the BVC at the College of Law in 1998 and is now on her first six-month pupillage. Why was Kim so determined to become a barrister?

'One of the options in my Institute of the Motor Industry exams focused on law and I've been fascinated by it ever since. The experiences of a friend who is a barrister also inspired me – what also appealed was the variety of work you deal with, being self-employed and the challenges that the Bar presents.'

Kim gave up her business to undertake a law degree at Middlesex University as a mature student. She was keen to gain experience from different sets of chambers. 'I prepared early and spent a lot of time during the third year of university applying for mini pupillages – I did 14 before

starting at the College of Law. It gave me the ideal opportunity to learn about different chambers, what kind of work they do and how they function.'

Kim chose to study the BVC at the college the first year the course was offered. 'The course was opening up to new providers and I wanted to be part of the innovative teaching methods that were being offered by the college. I also chose the College of Law because of its reputation in the legal community.'

The BVC was a challenge. The sheer volume of work and the fact that she was constantly learning so much made it hard, but also rewarding. 'Overall I really enjoyed the course. It was hard work, especially learning new skills such as drafting and opinion writing. Everything had a practical approach, which is different to most academic study. We also worked in small groups which was an excellent way to practise the new skills.'

FUNDING

Money is an extra hurdle. You'll need a fair amount of it to see you through since the fees alone for the BVC are around £6500–£7000. Those without a qualifying law degree will have an extra year's training to pay for when studying for the CPE or Diploma in Law. Only a limited number of awards, grants and scholarships are available for the vocational stage of Bar training. These include:

- Local authority grants
- Bank loans for professional studies
- Career Development Loans
- Chambers' pupillage awards – refer to *The Chambers Pupillage and Awards Handbook* for details
- Bar Council Scholarship Trust – further details from the Bar Council

SKILLS AND QUALITIES

- Good academic ability
- Flexibility and ability to adapt
- Written and verbal communication skills
- Numeracy
- Interpersonal skills
- Computer skills
- Professional conduct
- Confidence and independence
- Commercial awareness
- Meticulousness
- A lot of drive

...and many more.

CASE STUDY

Barrister

Andrea gained tenancy with her high-profile chambers in London in 1998. Recounting pupillage she says, 'I had a marvellous pupil master – he was really great. But every day you are running to stand still. It's exhausting to always try to appear competent and be on top of things.' She comments, 'It can be awkward at first not knowing what your role is and it's difficult to gauge if you're being helpful or not. It can be hard to work out what the general protocol is.' During her first three months she worked solely for her pupil master. After about four to five months she worked for anyone who needed her and they all had to report on her work. 'The hours are very irregular and I have to work many evenings and weekends,' she says.

'I am now a tenant which means I operate from chambers. I am officially self-employed but use the facilities of chambers, the clerks and the administrative support. As a tenant I pay chambers rent for these services. It's difficult at first when you become a tenant. Previously everyone was constantly scrutinising everything you did and now you are completely responsible for you own work.'

Andrea has a lot of variety in her work. She is involved in many County Court arbitrations and employment tribunals and has been working on a big commercial case. 'Initially the clerks have a bank of solicitors they put you in touch with. You need to keep your contacts going with a bit of proactive maintenance. At the beginning it is very random, then you tend to develop the solicitors you feel comfortable working with.

'To do this job you need to be the sort of person who has utter confidence in what you are doing – or at least appear to have! You are utterly vulnerable to the whims of the solicitor. You put your soul into a piece of work and need to be robust so as not to take it too personally. You need to have pride in wanting to look good in front of your peers and it can be quite a lonely way of working. You require the skills of being self-employed and a funny mixture of confidence and paranoia! You certainly have to be meticulous and have a lot of drive. The work is totally insecure and you have to adopt a sense of pragmatism.'

Andrea has an English Literature degree from Cambridge University. She did one year's voluntary work then joined the Civil Service Fast Stream for two years before leaving to do the CPE followed by the BVC. Her advice is 'Be prepared to put your life on hold, especially during pupillage. You'll lose touch with a lot of your friends because you can't make arrangements. You need to have an extraordinary mindset and not think beyond pupillage. It is also an excellent idea to do some mini-pupillages to test the water, even at places you don't want to go to.'

QUALIFYING AS AN ADVOCATE IN SCOTLAND

The intending advocate in Scotland needs to take an LLB degree followed by the postgraduate Diploma in Legal Practice plus one or two years training in Scotland in a solicitor's office. It is advised that intending advocates practise as solicitors for a period before going to the Bar. This is followed by further unpaid practical training called 'devilling' to an experienced advocate in combination with sitting the Faculty of Advocates' written examinations. Contact the Faculty of Advocates for further information. (See Chapter 11 for address.)

QUALIFYING AS A BARRISTER IN NORTHERN IRELAND

The Institute of Professional Legal Studies at the Queen's University of Belfast offers a one-year postgraduate course of vocational training for both trainee barristers and trainee solicitors. Anyone who intends to enter either branch of the legal profession in Northern Ireland must attend the Institute and successfully complete the course that leads to the award of the Certificate in Professional Legal Studies. Bar trainees spend a week work-shadowing a practising barrister immediately prior to commencing their course. A further period of in-practice training starts after graduation from the Institute and takes the form of a 12-month pupillage.

All applicants must hold a recognised law degree or hold a degree in any subject other than law and have successfully completed a course of legal study approved by the Council of Legal Education (Northern Ireland). For further information contact the Institute of Professional Legal Studies. (See Chapter 11 for address.)

INSTITUTIONS OFFERING THE BAR VOCATIONAL COURSE

- BPP Law School
- Cardiff Law School
- The College of Law (London)
- Inns of Court School of Law
- Manchester Metropolitan University
- University of Northumbria at Newcastle
- Nottingham Law School
- University of the West of England

Chapter 6
GETTING WORK EXPERIENCE

Getting work experience has become more and more significant in recent years and in a climate when obtaining a training contract or pupillage is so fiercely competitive, it is not enough to be purely a brilliant academic. The more experience (ideally relevant) that you have, the better your chance of succeeding.

WHAT HAVE YOU GOT TO GAIN FROM WORK EXPERIENCE?

- It will give you a good insight into the legal profession and whether or not that is what you want to do. Some real experience will be particularly useful if you are trying to weigh up the pros and cons of qualifying as a barrister or solicitor.

- It helps you to make a better transition into the world of full-time work.

- It gives you the opportunity to build up those all-important contacts.

- It will help you to gain excellent (hopefully!) references.

However, it is not that easy getting legal work experience. Most employers recognise this and do not stipulate that it is essential, although it is preferred. But if you can't get experience in a firm of solicitors or chambers, any work experience that demonstrates use of the skills they are interested in will be valuable. Skills such as communications skills, determination, business awareness, IT skills can all be developed in many other sectors of business and commerce.

WHAT ARE THE OPPORTUNITIES TO GAIN LEGAL WORK EXPERIENCE?

- Placement in a firm of solicitors
- Mini-pupillage in chambers
- Paralegals and outdoor clerks
- Barristers' clerk
- The Law Commission
- Law centres
- Citizens Advice Bureaux
- Voluntary work in charitable organisations

MARKETING YOURSELF

There is no one guaranteed way of succeeding in getting work experience, so try as many as you can think of and be creative in the process. Here are a few suggestions:

- Ask your teachers at school/college if they have any contacts in the legal profession.

- Use your careers service and speak to your careers officer.

- Talk to your family and friends and ask them if they can suggest anyone to contact.

- Make sure everyone you know is aware you are looking for work experience.

- Send your CV to firms of solicitors. *The Chambers and Partners Guide* will give you names and addresses of solicitors' firms.

- Send your CV to chambers. *The Chambers and Partners Guide* will give you names and addresses of chambers.

- Keep up to date with the profession by reading the 'quality press' on their relevant legal days and look at specialist journals such as *The Law Society Gazette* and *The Lawyer,* which should both be available at large public libraries.

Perhaps you could ask to go in for one or two weeks of work experience during the holidays or even ask for one day's work shadowing to get an insight into what the working environment is like. Whichever route you take will almost certainly be on a voluntary basis unless you have specific skills to offer, such as good office and keyboard skills. If you do have such skills, you could try to get some paid work with a firm of solicitors during the summer or register with an employment agency.

How to apply

It's never too early to start to put together a curriculum vitae (CV). A CV is a summary of what you have done in your life to date. If you have had very little work experience, one page on good quality A4 paper will be sufficient. If you are a mature student with a lot of jobs behind you there is a case for going on to a second page, but for most of you a one-page CV will be appropriate.

So what should go into your CV? Here are the main headings:

- Name

- Address and telephone number

- Date of birth

- Nationality

- Education and qualifications
  Start with your present course of study and work back to the beginning of secondary school. No primary schools please! List the qualifications with grades you already have and the exams you intend to sit.

- Work experience
  Start with the most recent. Don't worry if you've only had a Saturday job at the local shop or a paper round. Put it down. Employers would rather see that you've done something.

- **Skills**

  List those such as computer skills, software packages used, languages, driving licence.

- **Interests and positions of responsibility**

  What do you like to do in your spare time? If you are or have been captain of a sports team, been a committee member or even Head Boy or Girl at school, put it all down.

- **Referees**

  Usually two: an academic referee such as a teacher or head of your school, plus someone who knows you well personally, who is not a relative, such as someone you have worked for.

Always highlight your good points on a CV and don't leave gaps. Always account for your time. If something such as illness prevented you from reaching your potential in your exams, point this out in the covering letter (see page 51). Lawyers have excellent attention to detail so make sure your spelling and grammar are perfect!

A SAMPLE CV

There is no standard CV but here is a sample:

PERSONAL DETAILS

Name	Sandra Anthony TATE
Address	134 Hillhouse Avenue Portsmouth PO1 2TQ
Telephone No	01392 66455
Date of Birth	10 June 1981
Nationality	British

EDUCATION & QUALIFICATIONS

1993–1999	Linfield High School, Portsmouth
1999	A-levels: English (A), History (A), French (B)
	Eight GCSEs: English (A), Mathematics (B), History (A), Geography (C), Chemistry (B), Biology (B), French (A), Latin (A)

WORK EXPERIENCE

1995 & 1996	Delivering newspapers and magazines throughout my local area.
1997 & 1998	(Saturdays) Sales assistant in busy dry cleaners in centre of Portsmouth.
August 1998	Two weeks as temporary receptionist in small firm of accountants, responsible for answering telephones and general clerical work.

SKILLS

Languages – good written and spoken French.
Computing – competent in MS Word and Excel.

POSITIONS OF RESPONSIBILITY

Captain of squash team at school.

INTERESTS

Squash, swimming, reading (particularly biographies) and travelling to other countries such as America and France.

REFERENCES

Available on request.

THE COVERING LETTER

Every CV or application form should always be accompanied by a covering letter. The letter is important because it is usually the first thing a potential employer reads. Here are some tips:

■ The letter should be on the same plain A4 paper as your CV and should look like a professional document. No lined paper please! Use one side of A4 only.

■ Try to find out the name of the person you should send your letter and CV to. It makes a great difference to the reader the more you can personalise your application. If you start the letter 'Dear Mr Brown' remember you should finish it 'Yours sincerely'.

■ The first paragraph should tell the reader why you are contacting them.

■ The second paragraph should give them some information to make them interested in you, such as highlighting your interest in law along with some specific IT skills.

■ Say in the letter if you already know anything about the firm or have read anything in the press recently that is relevant.

■ Employers accept typed letters, unless they specifically request them to be handwritten (as some law firms prefer).

Chapter 7 CHOOSING YOUR UNIVERSITY COURSE

In the late 1980s, demand for trainee solicitors briefly exceeded supply. Virtually anyone could pick up a training contract (then called 'articles') if they had the necessary qualifications. These days, however, competition is tough and you'll need to show lots of ability and drive to impress your potential employers. The situation for budding barristers is similar.

But there is a positive side:

- Employers are generally impressed by a good calibre law graduate since law is known to be a challenging discipline requiring skills such as research, analysis, application, clarity, advocacy and effective written communication. These are very relevant in other jobs, so while on the one hand you don't need a law degree to enter the profession, but on the other, law can be your springboard into a wide range of career possibilities.

- Some parts of the legal profession are growing, with law firms becoming more international and opening offices overseas (particularly in Eastern Europe) and expanding in areas such as Environmental Law and Intellectual Property Law.

The road to qualifying as a barrister or solicitor may not be easy, but the professional rewards can be great. If you are undeterred and still have your heart set on a law degree in some shape or form, it's time to start thinking about your next steps.

WHAT TO CONSIDER

The basic criteria for choosing your degree course are:

1. the kind of law course you are after
2. where you want to study
3. your academic ability.

Going to university is an investment, so it is worth giving these points careful thought and research. From the growing number of institutions offering law courses you need to look at ways of narrowing your options.

Once you have eliminated the bulk of the institutions and courses on offer, start to carry out your own research:

- Contact your chosen universities or colleges and ask for their prospectuses (both official and alternative) and departmental brochures (if they exist) for more details. Remember that such publications are promotional and may be selective in the information they provide.

- Attend university open days if you can, and talk to former or current students. Try to imagine if you would be happy living for three years in that environment and address issues such as: Is it a campus or in a city? Will it allow you to pursue your interests?

- Talk to any legal practitioners you know and ask for their views on the reputations of different universities and courses.

- Visit the websites of the universities you are considering.

- Find out what academic criteria they are looking for and be realistic about the grades you are expecting. Your teachers at school or college will be able to advise you on this.

Once you have done this research, you should be able to make a shortlist of universities and from that you can choose the top six places to put down on the UCAS form.

SUGGESTED TIME-SCALE

Year 12

May/June:
Do some serious thinking. Get ideas from friends, relatives, teachers, books etc. If possible visit some campuses before you go travelling!

June/July/
August:
Make a shortlist of your courses.
Lay your hands on copies of the official and alternative (student-written) prospectuses and departmental brochures for extra details. They can usually be found in libraries but it's better to get your own sent to you. Look at the university departments' websites.

Year 13

September:
Fill out your application form and send it off to UCAS (via your referee) – it will be accepted from 1 September onwards.

15 October:
Deadline for applying for places at Oxford or Cambridge.

15 December:
Deadline for submitting your applications to UCAS. They will consider late applications, but your chances are limited since some of the places will have already gone.

November:
Universities hold their open days and sometimes interviews.

April:
Decisions will begin to be sent directly to the candidates.

By 15 May:
Or within two weeks of the final decision you receive, you must tell UCAS (assuming you've had some offers) which offer you have accepted firmly and which one is your back-up.

| Spring: | Fill out yet more forms – this time the grant forms which you can get from your school, college or LEA. |
| Summer: | Sit your exams and wait for the results. UCAS will get in touch by early September and tell you whether your chosen universities or colleges have confirmed your conditional offers. Don't be too disappointed if you haven't got in. Just get in touch with your school, college or careers office and wait until clearing starts in September when any left-over places are filled. You will be sent instructions on clearing automatically, but it's up to you to get hold of the published list of unfilled places and contact the universities directly. |

For more information about UCAS and filling in your application see *How to Complete Your UCAS Form* (see reading list in Chapter 11).

DIFFERENT KINDS OF LAW COURSE AVAILABLE

(a) Course content – Single or Joint Honours?

All the institutions listed in this guide on pages 29–37 offer qualifying law degrees as recognised by the Law Society and the Bar Council. This means that you can select the required courses that will exempt you from taking the Common Professional Examination (CPE) after you graduate. The seven foundations of legal knowledge are Contract, Tort (often both are referred to as Obligations), Criminal Law, Constitutional and Administrative Law (or Public Law), Property Law (or Land Law), Equity and Trusts and Law of the European Union.

Law can be taken on its own or mixed with a number of other subjects. It can be difficult to decide whether to study law by itself (a Single Honours degree), with another subject (Joint or Combined degree) or as part of a modular programme, alongside a multitude of topics.

If you are considering a Single Honours course a good range of optional subjects might make it even more inviting. You don't want to be stuck with just a handful of choices from which to fill in your timetable after you've put down the core courses. And options may be law related or from a completely different discipline. Some places can only offer a limited selection, while others provide a variety of law courses as well as the opportunities to take non-law courses.

Alternatively, if you want to specialise in one other area, then a Joint degree might be more appealing. Some Joint degrees do not require previous knowledge of the second subject. Others, especially those with a European language, often specify that candidates must have an A-level or GCSE for background knowledge. With Joint degrees, be wary of courses that have seemingly identical titles, for example, Law with German, Law and German, and Law and German Law. In the first one, law is the major subject; in the second, you'll probably spend equal time on each and in the third the emphasis is on law rather than German language. Any of them may involve some time abroad.

(b) Black letter, contextual and vocational approaches

It is worth knowing that there are broadly three different approaches to teaching law. But you cannot base your selection on this criteria since few institutions adhere to one kind. Most places are likely to opt for a mixture (sometimes even within an individual unit, especially if it is taught by several different tutors). It can be useful though to find out (perhaps during an open day) which attitude is prevalent. The categories are:

(i) Black Letter Law
This focuses on the core subjects and doesn't look much beyond statutes and legal reports for its sources of law. It may sound dry, but it should provide a thorough grounding in the English legal system.

(ii) Contextual Approach

Some courses examine law in context, that is to say law, its role and its effectiveness are looked at in relation to society (past and present), politics and the economy. Such courses may include elements of Critical Legal Theory. Students are expected to analyse the problems (for example, loopholes, contradictions, injustices and so on) within the law. And this can make for some heated and controversial seminars.

(iii) Vocational Approach

This stresses professional training and skills. It includes sandwich degrees with work placements and other degrees with units dedicated to lawyers' skills like negotiating, interviewing, counselling, drafting, research, analysis, clear expression and the ability to read through vast amounts of material, sift out the legally relevant points and present a logical argument. In fact, you will be able to pick up most of these skills through other standard law units and extracurricular activities like mooting (a mock court room trial), debating and law clinics, in which students get the opportunity to help out with a real-life case from start to finish.

(c) Studying overseas and work placements

Studying overseas and/or completing a work placement could also be factors affecting your degree selection. Not all of these courses will send you off for a full year though. Neither must you be a linguist, since you can study or work overseas in English in, for example, North America, the Netherlands or Malaysia. The availability of student exchanges has increased through programmes such as Erasmus, which encourage universities to provide international opportunities where practicable. There are relatively few law degree courses which insist on work placements; however, some hands-on experience during holidays will prove invaluable and you should try to organise this yourself, even if it is not a requirement of the course you choose. (See Chapter 6.)

WHERE YOU WANT TO STUDY

(a) Which country and legal system?

If you're hoping to practise law, ask yourself where you intend to work – England or Wales? Northern Ireland? Scotland? Since the legal systems differ across Britain, it seems pointless to study in Aberdeen if you want to practice in Aberystwyth. Although, if you do need to move it is usually possible to transfer the legal skills and knowledge you already have and adapt them to the new place. Note that all the degree courses listed on pages 29–37 are qualifying degrees for the purposes of practising in either England or Wales. There are other institutions in Scotland and Ireland, not covered here, which run degree courses that meet with the Scottish and Irish law societies' requirements, but are not recognised by the Law Society of England and Wales or the Bar Council.

(i) England and Wales
See Chapters 4 and 5.

(ii) Northern Ireland
Law in Northern Ireland is very similar to that in England and Wales, but if you wish to study in Ireland and want to practise over the water you are obliged to sit an additional exam in Land Law. In 1977 the Institute of Professional Legal Studies was set up at Queen's University in Belfast by the Council of Legal Education. The Council runs a course that provides training for law graduates wishing to become legal practitioners. This vocational course leads to a Certificate in Professional Legal Studies. The core subjects you need to start the course are the same as in England plus Company Law (or Law of Business Organisations) and Law of Evidence. But if you haven't already done these, you have to take a preliminary course for a Certificate in Academic Legal Studies. After these certificates you need to find a two-year apprenticeship to get your Restricted Practising Certificate so you can work as an assistant solicitor for a few years before becoming a fully qualified solicitor.

(iii) Scotland

Being a lawyer in Scotland (solicitor or advocate) initially involves passing a number of core subjects. The Faculty of Advocates and the Law Society specify eleven common subjects plus two more each. After taking these within your degree there comes a one-year postgraduate practical course: a Diploma in Legal Practice. Beyond this, budding solicitors need a two-year traineeship to be fully qualified and advocates are required to do additional practical training and exams.

(b) Various influencing factors

Once you've decided which country you'll be in, you can think about choosing specific institutions. But remember university life isn't going to be solely about academic study. It is truly a growing experience – educationally, socially, culturally – and besides, three or four years can really drag if you're not happy outside the lecture theatre. Below is an assortment of factors that might have some bearing on where you'd like to study. See which ones you think are relevant to you and try to put them in order of importance.

Academic and career-related factors

Educational facilities

Is there a well-stocked and up-to-date law library nearby, or will you have to fight other students for the materials? Check for access to computer terminals that you can use for improving the presentation of your dissertations, and availability of legal databases (such as Justis and Lexis). More vocational courses might use mock court rooms with video and audio equipment. Bear in mind that the facilities available will depend on the budget of an institution and plentiful resources tend to attract better tutors.

Quality of teaching

Difficult to establish without the benefit of an open day but the University Funding Council, an independent body set up by the government, has done the groundwork for you and assessed the level of teaching across the UK already. Its findings are publicly available from the External Relations Department, Higher Education Funding Council, Northaven House, Coldharbour Lane, Bristol BS16 1QD. Teaching quality may suffer if seminar or tutorial groups are too large, so try to compare group sizes for the same courses at different institutions.

Type of institution

There are basically three types:

- **The 'old' universities**
  Traditionally the more academic universities with higher admission requirements, the old universities are well established with good libraries and research facilities. They have a reputation for being resistant to change, but most are introducing modern elements into their degrees such as modular courses, an academic year split into two semesters and programmes like Erasmus.

- **The 'new' universities**
  Pre-1992 these were polytechnics or institutes. They form a separate group because they still hold true to the original polytechnic doctrine of vocational courses and strong ties with industry, typically through placements and work experience. They are still looked down upon by some employers because of their generally lower academic entry requirements, but the new universities have a good name for flexible admissions and learning, modern approaches to their degrees and good pastoral care. Some law courses at these new universities have been categorised as 'excellent' by the University Funding Council.

- **The colleges of higher education**
  Usually these are specialist institutions and therefore provide excellent facilities in their chosen fields despite their smaller size. They are sometimes affiliated to universities, such as Holborn

College and the University of Wolverhampton. This form of franchising means the college buys the right to teach the degree, which the university will award, provided that the course meets the standards set by the university.

Attractiveness to employers

Few employers will openly admit to giving preference to graduates from particular universities. Most are looking for high-quality degrees as an indication of strong academic ability. But since students with higher A-level grades have tended to go to the old universities, it is unsurprising that a large proportion of successful lawyers come from traditional university backgrounds.

Full time versus part time and distance learning

Although most students prefer to study full time and finish their degrees in the shortest time possible, some people, for a variety of reasons, find it more convenient to study part time or from home or via the Internet. Only a limited number of institutions offer these options.

Guaranteed place on LPC

Many universities have an arrangement with the College of Law which assures a place on an LPC to every student with a 2:2 degree or better. This is a good safety net if you fail to get a 2:1, but if you think you will have difficulty getting a good law degree before you even start, ask yourself if you wouldn't be happier and more successful studying another subject.

Non-academic considerations

■ **Finances**
The cost of living isn't the same throughout the UK, so will you be able to reach deeper into your pockets for rent or other fundamentals and entertainment if you are living in a major city or in the south?

- **Friends and family**
  Do you want to get away from them or stay as close as possible? While there can be advantages, financial at least, to living at home, you may prefer the challenge of looking after yourself and the opportunity to be completely independent.

- **Accommodation**
  Do you want to live on campus or in halls of residence with other students, or in private housing that you may need to organise yourself and that could be a considerable distance from college? If your university is nearby, is there any point in moving away from home?

- **Entertainment**
  Are you going to be spending much time in, for example, the sports centre, the theatre or student bars? How about university societies — is there one that allows you to indulge your existing hobbies or the ones you've always dreamt of trying?

- **Site and size**
  Not usually a problem, since many universities overcome the problems of urban *vs* rural and small *vs* large by locating their campus on the edge of a major town (eg University of Nottingham and University of Kent), and centralising certain facilities and services to ensure safety, convenience and some sense of community even on the largest and most widespread campus.

ACADEMIC ABILITY

For the majority of students, their A-level scores will be the deciding criteria for selection. And it's important to be realistic about the grades you're heading for: don't be too pessimistic, but don't kid yourself about your 'as yet undiscovered' genius. Talk to your teachers for an accurate picture of your predicted results.

Some places specify particular grades but will still take you on if you get the same point score. So, for example, if you are supposed to get ABC (which amounts to 10+8+6 = 24 points), then any combination which produces 24 points (ie BBB or AAD) may be acceptable.

Not one institution requires law A-level from potential students. Oddly, those of you with a little legal knowledge might even find yourself at a disadvantage. Few courses specify subjects they want you to have studied (with the exception of most language Joint degrees), although traditional qualifications are welcomed everywhere. Conversely, some universities won't accept A-levels like General Studies, or the less academic ones such as Art.

If your A-level results effectively prevent you from taking a law degree, it's time for a rethink. If you wanted to take a law degree with a view to entering the profession, then you could opt for the entry route with a non-law degree instead. Most employers stress that a large number of trainee solicitors and pupil barristers have a non-law degree. Even though the route might be longer and therefore more expensive (if sponsorship cannot be found), a graduate with, say, an upper second class Honours degree in Philosophy is infinitely more likely to make a successful lawyer than someone who scraped a pass in their LLB. It is important to remember that, since degree courses can change format frequently, you must check with universities directly to confirm their specific requirements.

Remember that if you intend to read a subject other than law you will have to complete, following graduation in that discipline, a one-year postgraduate conversion course in law (CPE/Postgraduate Diploma in Law) before going on to a Legal Practice Course or Bar Vocational Course.

Chapter 8
COMPLETING YOUR UCAS FORM

General advice on filling in your UCAS form is given in another guide in this series, *How to Complete Your UCAS Form*, by Tony Higgins, Chief Executive of UCAS (see the reading list in Chapter 11).

The following advice should help you complete Section 10, your personal statement. This is your opportunity to explain to the university admissions staff why you want to study law.

FILLING IN YOUR PERSONAL SECTION

The personal section of the UCAS form is the only chance you get to recommend yourself as a serious candidate worthy of a place, or at least, worthy of an interview. It is therefore vital that you think very carefully indeed about how to complete it so that it shows you in the best possible light. You must sell yourself to the department of law and make it hard for them not to take you.

For 1998 entry 21,273 applicants made 82,900 applications for a law degree, where law was the major area of study. Yet only 12,102 of those applicants were successful in being offered a place on a law degree. So you can understand how competitive applying for law is.

Obviously, there are as many ways of completing your Section 10 as there are candidates. There are no rules as such, but there are recommendations that can be made.

Universities are academic institutions so you must present yourself as a strong academic bet. The admissions tutor reading your form will want to know all the relevant information about you and will want some answers to the following questions.

- What is the strength of your commitment to academic study?

- Why do you wish to study law? Money, status, family traditions, enjoying the sound of your own voice , or fancying the idea of all that legal paraphernalia are not convincing reasons.

- What precisely it is about the law that interests you? Give details and examples referring to recent cases, controversies and debates.

- What do you hope to get out of three years of legal academic study?

- What legal cases have you followed in detail?

- What relevant material have you read recently and can you explain why you appreciated it?

- What recent judgments have you admired recently and why?

- What legal controversies have excited you?

- Which particular branch of the law interests you most and (again) why?

- Which lawyers (living or otherwise), have inspired you and for what reasons?

Work experience is very useful as it demonstrates a commitment to the subject outside the classroom. Remember to include any experience, paid or voluntary. If you have had relevant work experience, discuss it on your form. Explain concisely what your job entailed and what you got out of the whole experience. Even if you've not been able to get work experience, if you have spoken to anyone in the legal profession about their job it is worth mentioning as this all builds up a picture of someone who is keen and has done some research. Wanting to be Ally McBeal or Rumpole are not good enough reasons to convince a hardened admissions tutor of your commitment to a law degree!

Future plans, if any, should also be included on your form. Be precise. Again this will demonstrate a breadth of interest in the subject. For example, 'I am particularly interested in pursuing a career at the Bar. My enthusiasm was initially sparked off by my active participation in the Debating Society at school, of which I am President. I also follow the major legal cases in the newspaper and have visited the Old Bailey on a number of occasions.'

Other activities

At least half of your Section 10 should deal with material directly related to your chosen course. But the rest of the page should tell the admissions tutor all about what makes you who you are:

- What travel have you undertaken?

- What do you read?

- What sporting achievements do you have?

- What music do you like or play?

In all these areas give details.

> *'Last year I went to Paris and visited all the Impressionist galleries. I relax by reading American short stories – André Dubus and Raymond Carver among others. My musical taste is largely focused on opera (I have seen 14 productions of 'The Magic Flute') and I would like to continue playing the cello in an orchestra at university. I would also enjoy the chance to play in a football team to keep myself fit.'*

This is much more impressive than only saying:

> *'Last year I went to France. I like reading and listening to music and sometimes I play football at weekends.'*

GENERAL TIPS

- Take a photocopy of your personal statement so you can remind yourself of all the wonderful things you said about yourself, should you be called for interview!

- Do not add any additional pages.

- Make sure it's legible as the form will be reduced to half its original size before being passed to institutions.

- If you are planning to do so, state your reasons for applying for deferred entry and your plans for the year before entry. For example, you might be hoping to find some relevant work experience in a firm of solicitors followed by some time spent in Germany to brush up your German language conversation skills.

ELECTRONIC APPLICATION SYSTEM

Paper application forms could soon be a thing of the past as more and more schools turn to UCAS's Electronic Application System (EAS). This system has been available to all schools and colleges since 1998. The EAS allows you to fill in your UCAS application form on a personal computer at your school, college, local careers service, or even your PC at home. Your application is sent to UCAS on floppy disk or via the Internet. This alternative to the paper form has proved popular with both applicants and schools/colleges. Ask at your school or college for further details.

Chapter 9
SUCCEEDING AT INTERVIEW

THE ACADEMIC INTERVIEW

Outside Oxford and Cambridge formal interviews are rarely part of the admissions process. Even at highly respected institutions such as King's College London and University College London, interviews are not the norm for all candidates and are usually reserved for those from a non-traditional background and some mature candidates. They are expensive and time-consuming for both the university and the applicants. However, although academic interviews are rare, they do occur, so if you're invited to attend for interview, here are some points to bear in mind:

- Remember that if you shine in your interview and impress the admissions staff they may drop their grades slightly and make you a lower offer.

- Interviews need not be as daunting as you fear. They are designed to help those asking the questions to find out as much about you as they can. It is important to have good eye-contact and confident body language and view it as a chance to put yourself across well rather than as an obstacle course designed to catch you out.

- Interviewers are more interested in what you know than what you do not. If you are asked a question you don't know the answer to, say so. To waffle simply wastes time and lets you down. To lie, of course, is even worse, especially for aspiring lawyers!

- Remember your future tutor might be among the people interviewing you. Enthusiasm and a strong commitment to your subject and, above all, a willingness to learn, are extremely important attitudes to convey.

- An ability to think on your feet is vital... another prerequisite for a good lawyer. Pre-learned answers never work. Putting forward an answer, using examples and factual knowledge to reinforce your points, will impress interviewers far more. It is also sensible to admit defeat if your argument is demolished.

- It is possible to steer the interview yourself to some extent. If you are asked something you know nothing about, confidently replacing that question with another related one shows enthusiasm for and knowledge of the subject.

- Essential preparation includes revision of the personal section of your UCAS form, so don't include anything on your form you're unprepared to speak about at interview.

- Questions may well be asked on your extracurricular activities. Most often this is a tactic designed to put you at your ease and therefore your answers should be thorough and enthusiastic.

- At the end of the interview you'll probably be asked if there is anything you would like to ask your interviewer. If there is nothing, then say that your interview has covered all that you had thought of. It is sensible, though, to have one or two questions of a serious kind – to do with the course, the tuition and so on – up your sleeve. It is not wise, obviously, to ask them anything that you could and should have found out from the prospectus.

- Above all, end on a positive note and remember to smile!

PREPARATION FOR A LAW INTERVIEW

We are assuming that you will be taking a Single Honours Law degree, but if you have chosen a Joint or Combined Honours course you will have to prepare yourself for questions on those other subjects as well.

The interview is a chance for you to demonstrate knowledge of, commitment to and enthusiasm for the law. The only way to do this is to be extremely well informed. Interviewers will want to know your reasons for wishing to study law and, possibly above all, they will be looking to see whether you have a mind capable of developing logical arguments and the ability to articulate such arguments powerfully and coherently. Much of the practice of law in this country rests on an adversarial system, so don't be surprised if you receive an adversarial interview. Remember to keep calm and think clearly!

Reasons for wishing to study law vary. A passion for courtroom drama or popular TV programmes loosely based on legal practice is not enough. You need to think about the everyday practice of the law in this country and it is extremely useful to spend time talking with lawyers of all kinds and learning from them what is involved.

It is important to be aware of the many types of law that lawyers practise – criminal, contract, family, taxation, etc... and be clear about the differences between them. The essential differences between barristers and solicitors must also be clear in your mind.

Use of the media

As a serious A-level candidate you should already be reading a 'quality' daily newspaper. *The Independent, The Times* and *The Guardian* all have law sections during the week. If you are really keen, read the *Law Society Gazette* or *The Lawyer,* which are published weekly. Following detailed law reports in the press will give you further insight into the ways in which the law is practised.

Regular listening to the radio and watching television are vital. Much of the news has legal implications and these subjects are consistently discussed in the broadcast media. TV's 'Question Time', 'Newsnight' and certain 'Panorama' style documentaries and radio's 'The Today Programme', 'The World this Weekend' and 'Today in Parliament' are all examples of potentially very useful programmes to help you build up a thorough knowledge of current events. Also regularly visit the legal websites mentioned in Chapter 11.

Knowledge of the structure of the legal and judicial systems is vital. You should know who the Lord Chief Justice is, who the Director of Public Prosecutions is and what he or she does. You should be aware of recent controversial legal decisions, who took them and what their consequences are or could be. Who is the Home Secretary and why is he or she important? What do you think should be happening in the prison system at the moment? What reforms would you like to see implemented in the running of the police force?

The interview

Interviewers will ask questions that will help them form an opinion about the quality of your thought and your ability to argue a particular case. You may be presented with a real or supposed set of circumstances and be asked to comment on their legal implications. Is euthanasia wrong? What is the purpose of prison?

Recent events are very likely to form a large part of the interview. Ethical issues, political issues, police issues, prison reform issues – all of these are possible as the basis for questions at interview. An ability to see the opposite point of view while maintaining your own will mark you out as strong law degree material.

Don't forget that interview skills are greatly improved by practice. Chat through the issues we have discussed with your friends and then arrange for a teacher, careers officer or family friend to give you a mock interview.

THE INTERVIEW FOR WORK EXPERIENCE

Most of the above-mentioned tips would equally apply if you are going for an interview for work experience to a firm of solicitors or a set of chambers. However, you should also:

■ Research the firm/chamber thoroughly before interview. Look at their brochure and website.

- Plan in advance what you think your key selling points are to the employer and make sure you find an opportunity in the interview to get your points across.

- Prepare a few questions to ask your interviewer about the firm at the end. You can demonstrate your preparation here by asking them about something you have read about the firm/chambers recently, if appropriate.

- Dress smartly and appropriately. Lawyers tend to look quite formal.

- Remember to give a firm, confident handshake at the beginning and end of the interview.

POSSIBLE INTERVIEW QUESTIONS

Questions may be straightforward and specific, but they can range to the vague and border on the seemingly irrelevant. Be prepared for more than the blindingly obvious, 'Why do you want to study law?' question. But remember you wouldn't have been invited for interview unless you were a serious candidate for a place... so be confident and let your talents shine through! Here's a selection of typical interview questions for you to think about.

— Have you spoken to any lawyers about their work? Have you visited any courts?

— What makes a good judge/barrister/solicitor?

— What area of law are you interested in?

— What is the difference between the Laws of Contract and Tort?

— Have you read about any cases recently?

— Should cannabis/euthanasia be legalised?

— What are the pros and cons of fusing the two branches of the legal profession?

— Should the police in this country be armed?

— If you were in a position of power, would you change the current civil legal aid situation?

— Should the police spend their time enforcing the laws concerned with begging?

— Why are some juvenile offenders 'sent on holiday'?

— What are your views on the handling of the Stephen Lawrence case?

— Should Britain or any other country be intervening in situations like Kosovo?

— What are your views on the right to silence?

— How can you quantify compensation for victims of crime?

— Should criminals be allowed to sell their stories as 'exclusives'?

— Is it 'barbaric' to cane someone for vandalising cars?

— How does the law affect your daily life?

— What would happen if there were no law?

— Is it really necessary for the law to be entrenched in archaic tradition, ritual and jargon?

— How are law and morality related?

— Do you believe that all people have equal access to justice?

— What is justice?

— Why do we send criminals to prison? What are the alternatives?

— Should the media be more careful with the way in which they report real crime?

— Is law the best way to handle situations like domestic violence/child abuse/rape?

- Should British law encompass the laws of ethnic minorities since this society is so multicultural?

- What in your opinion are the causes of increased crime rates?

- Should trial by jury be more or less common?

- Do you think capital punishment should be reinstated?

- Would the law in this country be any different if there was no Royal family?

- You are driving along a busy road with the window down, when a swarm of bees flies into your car. You panic and lose control of the car causing a huge pile-up. Are you legally responsible?

- A blind person, travelling by train, gets out at his or her destination. Unfortunately the platform is shorter than the train, and the blind person falls on to the ground, sustaining several injuries. Who, if anyone, can compensate him or her?

Chapter 10
THE ENGLISH LEGAL SYSTEM

THE COURT STRUCTURE

The court structure is divided into two systems, those courts with civil jurisdiction and those with criminal jurisdiction.

Most cases are heard, in the first instance, by the County Court, but in cases where large amounts are in dispute, they will initially be heard in the High Court. Appeal from both the County Courts and the High Court is to the Court of Appeal (Civil Division).

All minor criminal matters are dealt with by the Magistrates Court. Serious cases are referred to the Crown Court. Here, the case will be decided upon by a lay jury, the essential element of the Common Law system. Cases can be appealed from the Magistrates Court to the Crown Court and from there to the Court of Appeal (Criminal Division).

The highest court in the land, not only for England and Wales, but also for Scotland and Northern Ireland, is the House of Lords, which only considers appeals in points of law. Each case is normally heard by five Law Lords in committee.

When a court is considering a European Community law point it may refer to the European Court of Justice in Luxembourg for interpretation.

JUDGES

By contrast with many other European countries, the judiciary in England and Wales is not a separate career. Judges are appointed from both branches of the legal profession. They serve in the House of

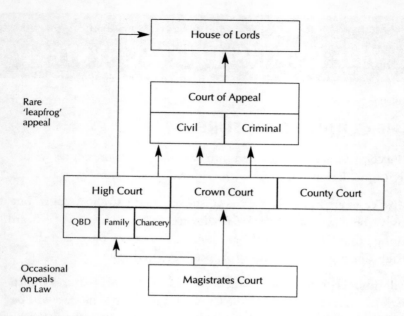

Outline of court structure

Lords, the Court of Appeal, the High Court and Crown Court or as Circuit or District Judges.

The Circuit Judges sit either in Crown Courts to try criminal cases or in County Courts to try civil cases. District Judges sit in County Courts. There are also part-time Judges appointed from both branches of the practising legal profession, who serve in the Crown Court, County Court or on various tribunals, for instance those dealing with unfair dismissal from employment.

In fact, most cases are dealt with not by Judges but by lay people, who are appointed to various tribunals because of their special knowledge, experience and good standing. For instance, the majority of minor criminal cases are judged by Justices of the Peace in Magistrates Courts. They are not legally qualified or paid but are respected members of the community who sit as magistrates part time.

All members of the judiciary are appointed by the Lord Chancellor, who is a member of the government and also speaker of the House of Lords. The Lord Chancellor holds a function similar to that of a Minister of Justice, although some matters concerning the administration of justice are the responsibility of the Home Secretary.

Once appointed, Judges are completely independent of both the legislature and the executive, and so are free to administer justice without fear of political interference.

LEGAL TERMINOLOGY

Administrative Law

This is one of the core (or exemption) courses needed for a qualifying law degree. It usually teams up with Constitutional Law. And it looks at the legal position of the government, public and local authorities and others who wield some kind of power over broadly defined policy, such as town planning and public health.

Black Letter Law

Means the fundamental areas of law like Law of Contract and Equity and Trusts. Doesn't include the more obscure or ephemeral law courses such as Feminist Perspectives in Law or Philosophy of Law. Tends only to examine law found in the law reports and statute books.

Civil Law

Unfortunately this has several meanings. It can refer to Roman Law but it is more likely to mean either (a) Private Law, ie all law other than Criminal, Administrative, Military and Church Law, or (b) the system of law which grew from Roman Law, as opposed to the English system of Common Law.

Clinical Legal Education

This is the opportunity for you to get some hands-on experience with real life cases without being able to go hideously wrong. Students, under supervision from qualified practitioners, give free legal advice to clients and usually see a case right through from beginning to end.

Common Law

This started about a thousand years ago in Britain. Until then, different localities had their own practices for dealing with problems and misdemeanours. Common Law was an attempt to iron out inconsistencies between different areas (basically so the men at the top could ensure their incomes and maintain their power) by applying one set of rules to similar circumstances.

Common Professional Examination (CPE)

The one-year course that non-law graduates must take to get on to the Legal Practice Course, on the road to becoming a solicitor. The fees alone are over £4000. You can avoid it by making sure you fit all the six core courses into your degree. (See core subjects on next page.)

Constitutional Law

The rules that control what the Crown, judiciary, Parliament and government do in relation to the country and all the individuals within it. But the Constitution of the UK remains largely unwritten, unlike most other states, and comprises statutes, Common Law rules and Constitutional Conventions.

Contract Law (Law of Contract)

There is an area of overlap between the Laws of Tort and Contract. The same set of circumstances can even lead to tortious or contractual actions, so look up Tort as well. Also, get used to this sort of far-fetched question: Adam has a TV which he promises to sell to Brian. Before he gets the telly though, Brian arranges to sell it to Chris for a tidy profit. However, Adam changes his mind about the deal with Brian and sells it to David instead. When David receives the TV, it has been badly damaged in transit so he calls Adam to complain. Adam directs David to the small print at the bottom of the receipt that passes all responsibility on to the haulier, and so on...

Who owns the TV and who should pay for the repairs? Yes, this is the kind of thing that tutors dream up to antagonise their students. It is an example of the law covering contracts, ie legally binding agreements (written, verbal or even implied) between two or more parties coming about as a result of offer and acceptance although there are several other criteria that must be fulfilled too.

Core Subjects

Currently these are: Constitutional and Administrative Law; Contract and Tort; Criminal Law; Equity and Trusts; the Law of the EC; and Property Law. They make up a qualifying law degree that will exempt you from the CPE course after you graduate.

CPE

See Common Professional Examination.

CPS

See Crown Prosecution Service.

Criminal Law

One of the cores. Crime is so often sensationalised that Criminal Law needs little introduction, but a lot of explanation, since the media continually obscure the legal points with hype. The law basically defines those acts that are seen to be public wrongs and are therefore punishable by the state. Most crimes are made up of two elements – the act itself *(actus reus)* and the thinking behind it (the *mens rea*), both of which must be proved 'beyond reasonable doubt' in court to establish guilt.

Crown Prosecution Service (CPS)

Born in 1986, the CPS, headed by the Director of Public Prosecutions, is responsible for virtually all the criminal proceedings brought in by the police in England and Wales, although the lawyers within the CPS don't always bring a case to court.

Delict Law (Law of Delict)

Simply the Scottish name for Tort.

DPP

Director of Public Prosecutions. See Crown Prosecution Service.

EC

European Community.

Equity

Half of the double act Equity and Trusts and one of the exemption courses. It is a (still developing) body of legal principles. And it originated in the Middle Ages when, if you felt the Common Law was letting you down, you could petition the King's Chancellor for a fair appraisal of the situation. The Chancellor was keen to see justice done and wasn't too bothered about the rigidity of the law. Even now, Equity prevails over the rules of law, but the system of Equity is no longer as arbitrary as before. The main areas of Equity cover trusts, property and remedies (eg injunctions). Look up the 'Anton Piller' order that is a more recent example of Equity at work.

Evidence

Remember that Tom Hanks film where the plot hinges on whether or not it's OK to use a crucial piece of evidence in court? Well, he lied in 'The Bonfire of the Vanities', and it was the Law of Evidence that he broke. This law covers the presentation of facts and proof in court. It is often associated with hearsay evidence that isn't always admissible, but also covers topics like confessions and the credibility of witnesses.

Exemption Subjects

See Core Subjects.

Jurisprudence

This is essentially the philosophy and theories of law. Jurisprudence units get right down to grass-roots level and usually examine law from a number of angles, such as Natural Law, Marxism and the Critical School.

Justis
This is a legal database giving you access to law-related information on computer. It is very similar to Lexis and Lawtel.

Land Law (Property Law)
No points for guessing that this looks at who has rights (equitable and real) in different types of property and how these rights or responsibilities may be established or transferred. It covers subjects like mortgages, trusts, landlords and tenants, leases, easements and covenants.

Law School
Simply refers to the law departments within universities. Not to be confused with College of Law where students study their LPC.

Lawtel
See Justis.

Lexis
See Justis.

LPC
Legal Practice Course – the vocational one-year course after graduation for those with a qualifying degree and prior to the two-year training contract, designed for intending solicitors. Those with a non-law degree will take the CPE before the LPC.

Moot
This is a mock court room trial. Some universities have specially made rooms for that really authentic feel, and others even go as far as to include video cameras to record your performance! But on the whole,

moots are organised as extracurricular/optional activities to improve
your confidence and help develop your legal skills of presenting a
clear, logical argument and questioning a witness.

Obligations (Law of Obligations)

This is just another name for the Laws of Tort and Contract.

Private Law

These are those bits of the law that are concerned with the relations
between individuals that really have nothing to do with the state, but
that doesn't stop the state intervening in certain circumstances, of
course. The areas are Family Law, Property Law and Trusts, Contract
and Tort.

Property Law

See Land Law.

Public Law

Sometimes this is the core course Constitutional and Administrative
thinly disguised. Although, strictly speaking, Public Law also
includes areas like Tax Law and Criminal Law since they too are
concerned with the relationship between the state and individuals.

Statute

A general word for a law passed by Parliament.

Statute Book

The list of all statutes that are currently in force.

Substantive Law

Virtually all universities put most of the emphasis on Substantive Law
at the undergraduate level. It is simply that huge part of the law that
deals with duties and rights and everything else that does not fall into
the category of practice and procedure.

Tort

Imagine it's a hot August day. You're gasping for a drink so you go into a café with your friend who buys you a bottle of beer. As you refill your glass you spot something a little suspicious and on closer inspection realise it's the decomposed remains of a snail! Do you...

(a) Drink the beer?

(b) Tell your friend to ask for a refund?

(c) Kick up a real furore and bring an action in tort against the manufacturer for negligence in production causing you to suffer shock and an upset stomach?

If your name was Mrs Donoghue and the year was 1928 then you'd go for option (c) and win the case – marking a milestone for the tort of negligence in English Law. They are largely concerned with providing compensation for people who have been wronged and suffered personal injury or damage to their property through negligence, defamation, nuisance, intimidation etc.

Training Contract

The name given to the two years after an LPC when you train as a kind of apprentice solicitor. In some cases, you can reduce the time spent by completing work placements as part of an undergraduate degree. But even then the training contract will last a minimum of one and a half years.

Trusts

See Equity. Taking the simplistic approach, trusts arise when someone transfers property to you but you can't use it. This is because the property is held on your behalf by trustees until you're 18. The property is entrusted to these trustees until you are able to choose to dissolve the trust and look after – or spend – the property yourself.

Chapter 11
FINDING OUT MORE

USEFUL ADDRESSES

Solicitors
The Law Society
50–52 Chancery Lane, London WC2A 1SX
Tel: 0171 242 1222; www.lawsociety.org.uk; www.lawsoc.org.uk

Barristers
The General Council of the Bar
3 Bedford Row, London WC1R 4DB
Tel: 0171 242 0082; www.barcouncil.org.uk

The Education & Training Officer
The General Council of the Bar
2/3 Cursitor Street, London EC4A 1NE
Tel: 0171 440 4000

Inns of Court
Gray's Inn, London WC1R 5EG
Tel: 0171 458 7900

The Inner Temple
London EC4Y
Tel: 0171 797 8250; www.innertemple.org.uk

Lincoln's Inn
London WC2A 3TL
Tel: 0171 405 0138; www.lincolnsinn.org.uk

The Middle Temple
London EC4Y 9AT
Tel: 0171 427 4800

Legal Action Group
242 Pentonville Road, London N1 9UW

Institute of Legal Executives
Kempston Manor, Kempston, Bedford MK42 7AB
Tel: 01234 841000; www.ilex.org.uk

Crown Prosecution Service
Personnel Branch
50 Ludgate Hill, London EC4M 7EX
Tel: 0171 273 8301; www.cps.gov.uk

The Law Society of Scotland
26 Drumsheugh Gardens, Edinburgh EH3 7YR
Tel: 0131 225 2934; www.lawscot.org.uk

The Faculty of Advocates
Advocates Library, Parliament House, Edinburgh EH1 1RF
Tel: 0131 226 5071

Institute of Professional Legal Studies
10 Lennox Vale, Malone Road, Belfast
Tel: 01232 245133; www.qub.ac.uk/ipls

The Law Society of Northern Ireland
98 Victoria Street, Belfast BT1 3JZ
Tel: 01232 231614

USEFUL BOOKS

The legal profession

There are vast numbers of books written about the law and the legal profession and new ones are constantly being published. It is worth a trip to your school library, local public library and careers office to check what is available. Here are some that might be useful to you:

Ivanhoe Career Guide to the Legal Profession, Cambridge Market Intelligence. An overview of the legal profession.
Legal Profession, CSU. The options from graduation to qualification.
GTI Law Journal, GTI. Practical information about life as a solicitor or barrister, written by practitioners.
Law Casebook, Hobsons. An overview of career options in law.
Career Opportunities in the International Legal Field, The Law Society. Opportunities for qualified lawyers and law graduates worldwide.
Solicitors' & Barristers' National Directory, The Law Society.
The Chambers & Partners Guide to the Legal Profession, Chambers & Partners Publishing. An annual comprehensive directory of firms of solicitors and barristers' chambers.
The Legal 500, by John Pritchard, Legalease. A detailed account of the UK legal profession.
Solicitors' Regional Directory: Your Guide to Choosing a Solicitor, The Law Society. A list of every firm in practice by region and town.
The Guide to Work Experience for intending Lawyers, GTI. Information on getting vacation placements and mini-pupillages.
The Bar Directory, FT Law & Tax. Details of chambers and barristers.
Chambers Pupillages & Awards Handbook, GTI, Details of chambers in England and Wales offering pupillages.
Prospects Legal, Central Services Unit.

General books on higher education

Degree Course Offers, Brian Heap, annual, Trotman.

Entrance Guide to Higher Education in Scotland, Committee of Scottish
   Higher Education Principals.
Getting into Oxford and Cambridge, Trotman.
Getting into University and College, Trotman.
How to Choose Your Degree Course, Brian Heap, annual, Trotman.
How to Complete Your UCAS Form, Tony Higgins, annual, Trotman.
Student Book, Klaus Boehm and Jenny Lees-Spalding (eds), annual,
   Trotman.
Students' Money Matters, Gwenda Thomas, Trotman.
UCAS Handbook, annual, UCAS.
University and College Entrance: The Official Guide, annual, UCAS.

FURTHER READING

General Books on Law
There are a number of good introductory texts on English Law and the
processes of learning the law. Among the ones we recommend are:

An Introduction to Law, P Harris, Butterworths, 1993.
Learning Legal Rules, JA Holland & JS Webb, Blackstone Press, 1996.
Learning Legal Skills, S Lee & M Fox, Blackstone Press, 1991.

Miscarriages of Justice
More Rough Justice, P Hill & M Young, Penguin, 1986.
Presumed Guilty: The British Legal System Exposed, M Mansfield,
   Heinemann, 1993.
Standing Accused, M McConville *et al*, Clarendon Press, 1994.
Report of the Royal Commission on Criminal Justice, Runciman
   Commission, HMSO, 1993.
Justice in Error, C Walker & K Starmer (eds), Blackstone Press, 1993.

Trial by Jury
Jury Trials, J Baldwin & M McConville, Oxford University Press, 1979.
Justice in Error, C Walker & K Starmer (eds), Blackstone Press, 1993.
A Matter of Justice, M Zander, Oxford University Press, 1989.

Civil Legal Aid

Smith & Bailey on the Modern English Legal System, SH Bailey & MJ
    Gunn, Sweet & Maxwell, 1991.
Achieving Civil Justice, R Smith (ed), Legal Action Group, 1996.
Tomorrow's Lawyers, PA Thomas (ed), Blackwell, 1992.

Professional Journals

Commercial Lawyer. A monthly magazine.
The Lawyer. A weekly newspaper for solicitors and barristers.
    http://www.the-lawyer.co.uk
The Law Society Gazette. Available from the Law Society.
Legal Business. Available from Legalease.
Legal Action. Bulletin of the Legal Action Group.
The Economist.

National Press

The Times (Tuesday), *The Independent* (Wednesday).

USEFUL LEGAL WEBSITES

You may already be very familiar with the Internet, and if you've not
yet explored the joys of 'surfing' it is a tool you will become
increasingly familiar with throughout the course of your studies and
working life. Here are some useful additional legal sites. Note that
addresses may change.

The College of Law
www.lawcol.org.uk

GTI – legal publishers
www.gti.co.uk

Legalease – legal publishers
www.legalease.co.uk

Butterworths – legal publishers
www.butterworths.co.uk

Information for Lawyers – a vast selection of links and information
www.infolaw.co.uk

Online Law – a huge database of information on firms and chambers
www.online-law.co.uk

Prospects Legal
www.prospects.csu.ac.uk

Semple Piggot Rochez – a virtual law school on the web
www.sppa.co.uk